In His Name

WEEKLY WORSHIP

Rev. Russell B. Greene, Jr.

DEDICATED

TO

My Devoted Wife,

MARION A. GREENE

My Grandmothers,

ANNA L. GREEN

And

KATHERINE A. HOUGHTON

My Mother,

RUTH H. GREENE

My Sisters,

ESTHER R. CONKLIN

And

LOIS P. VAN BUREN

My Mother-in-law,

ASLAUG E. ANDERSEN

ACKNOWLEDGEMENTS

It is with sincere and heartfelt gratitude that I acknowledge my daughter, Wendy Carter, for playing a vital role in the completion of this book.

CONTENTS

About This Book

My grandmothers, my mother, my two sisters, and my mother-in-law were at one time residents of various nursing homes. How well I remember the disappointment they conveyed to me whenever the weekly Worship Service was not held. Countless homebound Christians have expressed this same disappointment to me during my 53 years in the Parish Ministry. The same can be said for parishioners who often travel or have moved to locations without nearby services.

Effort is made to conduct weekly Worship Services for residents of nursing homes or homebound individuals, but far too many are being neglected. Volunteers are difficult to find to perform this ministry. They simply feel they are not qualified. Hence, there remain endless spiritual cravings that are not being satisfied.

This book has been written for this reason. It is a tool that enables anyone who can read to become qualified to conduct the weekly Worship Services of which we speak.

It is hoped these Worship Services will be conducted in nursing homes, private homes, hospitals, and the like by laypeople.

It is hoped that loved ones or others who care will be encouraged to assist in this manner, whenever and wherever the need arises.

It is recommended that a Bible and hymnal be available in order to read the suggested scripture lessons and hymns. Favorite hymns employed at the beginning and conclusion of these Worship Services would contribute much toward inducing a proper atmosphere.

Our Lord is available to all of us. Here is a simple and wonderful avenue to Him.

SUGGESTIONS

The following may be used in each of the Worship Services:

1) The OPENING may begin with the words:

   "Grace be unto you, and Peace from God our Father and Jesus Christ our Lord and Savior."

2) The HYMNS are suggested based on the content of the Weekly Word.

3) The SCRIPTURE may be announced as follows: "Hear the Words of the Lord as recorded in the Book of _____, verses_____."

4) The PRAYER may be concluded as follows:

   "We ask these things — whatsoever other things we should have asked — and what things that are now in our heart. In the name of Jesus, who taught us to say when we pray: Our Father, who art in Heaven, hallowed be Thy name. Thy Kingdom come, Thy will be done, on earth as it is in Heaven. Give us this day our daily bread, and forgive us our trespasses, as we forgive those who trespass against us. And lead us not into temptation, but deliver us from evil. For Thine is the Kingdom, the Power and the Glory, forever and ever. Amen."

5) The CLOSING may conclude with the words:

   "Now may the Lord bless you and keep you. The Lord make his face shine upon you and be gracious unto you. The Lord lift up his countenance upon you and give you peace. Amen."

A Lesson from Children

Hymn: "I Think, When I Read That Sweet Story of Old"

Scripture Lesson: Matthew 18:1-4

Sermon: "A Lesson from Children"

One afternoon, I received a telephone call from a resident of a nearby nursing home. I was asked if I could come to the home immediately. Upon my arrival, I found the resident in her wheelchair, watching for me. One quick glance revealed that she was in great distress. I wheeled her to her room. Upon entering the room, she handed me a religious publication. On the front cover was printed: "Whosoever does not receive the Kingdom of God like a child, shall not enter it."

The troubled woman pointed to the Bible verse and asked, "What does this mean? Does it mean I will not enter God's eternal Kingdom?"

I realized the elderly woman had interpreted the Bible passage to read: "Unless you are a child, you cannot enter the Kingdom." After explaining the verse to her, her worried face gave way to an expression of relief.

Upon leaving the nursing home, I couldn't help but think to myself how much happier we would be if we were more concerned with the meaning of this Bible verse.

The incident involving Jesus and the little children is certainly a familiar one. It is recorded in three of the four Gospels.

Let us take a moment to review this incident as recorded. Some followers came to Jesus, bringing small children so he could place his hands upon them and pray for them. The disciples made every effort to discourage this. When Jesus saw what the disciples were attempting to do, he stopped them. He told his disciples that they must let the little children come to him. "For the Kingdom of God is made up of little ones like these. [...] Truly, I assure you, the man who does not accept the Kingdom of God like a little child, will never enter it." Then, he took the children in his arms, laid his hands upon them, and blessed them.

The disciples felt the Master was too important and busy to be disturbed by children. However, Jesus seized this opportunity to reveal unto them what an opportunity this was.

This story has a twofold lesson.

First, the Lord conveys how vital it is to bring children to him, so they might begin to receive his blessings, especially at a young age. Their minds can be distorted and injured so easily. Their lives can be influenced and shaped by this ungodly world. Television, internet, and friends are constantly exerting influence; much of it not good.

Secondly, Jesus reveals that unless we have childlike faith, we shall not enter the Kingdom. In essence, the Master uses childhood to define the entrance requirements for the Kingdom. The child has the characteristics that make a solid foundation for the right relationship with the Heavenly Father.

Consider how quickly children surrender to the ways of the Lord. They are so eager to learn about him; so anxious to receive what he gives. They know they cannot go it alone, and therefore are very dependent. They are swift to believe and slow to distress. They are creatures of confidence instead of doubt; creatures of truth instead of hypocrisy; creatures of humility instead of pride. They are gentle and loving. They are innocent and slow to do evil. They are happy and carefree. They are delighted to hear Bible stories, enthusiastic about attending Sunday school, sincere in their prayers, and excited about getting to the work of the Kingdom.

Indeed, the world would be a much better place if we were more like our children.

My friends, Jesus does not tell us to be childish. He does not say that unless you are a child, you cannot enter the Kingdom. He simply tells us to have childlike faith. He tells us to cultivate and nourish the childlike spirit, and we shall be richly blessed.

Jesus says, “Whoever does not receive the Kingdom of God like a little child, shall not enter it.”

Prayer:

Heavenly Father, who through Your Son Jesus has taught us we must be as little children in order to enter Your Kingdom, fill us with Your Holy Spirit. Give us a childlike faith so our relationship with You might be pleasing in Your sight. Make us aware of our dependence upon You. Make us commend our lives into Your hands. Make us eager to learn of Your love. Make us delight in hearing Your Word. Make us sincere in our prayers. Make us swift to believe and slow to distrust. Make us creatures of confidence instead of doubt; truth instead of hypocrisy; humility instead of pride. Make us gentle and loving. Whatever our anxieties and afflictions, make us happy and confident, knowing You are our Shepherd, and we are the sheep of Your pasture. AMEN

(For the continuation of this Prayer, see "PRAYER" on page 2 in the Suggestions segment)

Hymn: "Lord, Dismiss Us with Thy Blessing"

Are You Confused?

Hymn: "O Come, O Come, Emanuel"

Scripture Lesson: Isaiah 40:1-5

Sermon: "Are you confused?"

It had been a long uphill road for Moses. Now, his journey through life was about to end. It had been a journey which practically began in a basket of bulrushes floating upon the Nile River — a journey which was to be completed only a short distance from the promised land of milk and honey.

Knowing he had little time, Moses was anxious about what might happen to his people after his departure. He knew their weaknesses. He knew they could be easily misled. There was so very much he wanted to tell the Israelites.

He, therefore, summoned his people to assemble around him. He then proceeded to remind the Israelites they were the children of God. As God's children, they should make every effort possible to be upright in conduct and unpolluted in worship. Their sole aim in life should be living lives pleasing to their Creator. To fulfill their calling, they would have to avoid the worldly ways and customs that dominated the land they were soon to enter. Moses cautioned his people against the contagious idolatrous practices of the Canaanites. He warned the Israelites that false teachers and prophets would continuously tempt them to oppose God's Holy Will. He said, “You shall not turn to these false teachers and prophets.”

The Israelites became troubled. If Moses was no longer to be among them, how would they know their Creator’s will? Shortly, they would become confused concerning which teachers and prophets they ought to give their attention.

In order that they might know God's Will and be spared any such confusion, Moses said unto his people, as recorded in the 18th chapter of Deuteronomy, verse 15, "The Lord your God will raise up for you a prophet like me. He shall come from among you. Listen to Him and the words he speaks."

The Lord God will raise up a prophet like Moses. Before we can become familiar with the prophet of whom Moses speaks, it is necessary to become better acquainted with Moses. Moses was extremely close to his people. Inasmuch as he was one of them, he was aware of their needs and problems. He was tempted by the same temptations. He ate and drank the same food and water.

The Almighty God had called Moses to serve as his special and unique instrument. God had freed the Israelites from their slavery in Egypt, where they had endured bondage for approximately 430 years. Through Moses, God had guided and directed and sustained the Israelites during their wilderness journey. Through Moses, the Lord God had revealed his Fatherly concern and love for his children.

Moses made every effort to bring his people into a right relationship with their Creator and into a right relationship with one another. He emphasized the holiness of the Lord and their own ungodliness. He attempted to preserve his people from error and to prepare their minds for future developments regarding the Kingdom of God. Again and again, he warned the Israelites concerning the perils of their wickedness and opposition to their Creator. He had pity for the penitent and deep, heartfelt feeling for the wayward. He interceded for his people whenever the need arose. Although many were in darkness concerning God's will, Moses reportedly gave them light.

Indeed, to his people, Moses was a leader and guide, a deliverer and mediator, a law giver and interpreter. He was the mouthpiece for God and the revealer of the Divine.

Truly, Moses played a prominent and remarkable role in the lives of the Heavenly Father's children. If it had not been for Moses, the Israelites would have surely perished.

And now, knowing he would soon depart, Moses said unto his people: "The Lord your God will raise up for you a prophet like me. He shall come from among you. Pay heed to what He tells you."

As you are well aware, many prophets appeared on the scene during the history of the Israelites. Whenever the need arose, whenever his children encountered confusion and darkness, God sent them a prophet. Were any of these prophets the prophet of whom Moses spoke? They were not, for the simple reason they also spoke of the Lord God sending his children a great prophet — of sending more than a prophet. They spoke of the Heavenly Father giving His children a Messiah. So down through the years, the children of Israel waited and looked for the Promised One.

Then finally, on that first Christmas morning many years ago, the prophecy of Moses and the other prophets was fulfilled in the person of Jesus Christ. And truly, Jesus was more than a prophet. He was God Himself. Through the person of Jesus Christ, God made Himself known unto mankind, once and for all time.

The example, given unto us by Jesus Christ, became a glorious revelation as to what is involved in the proper relationship between man and God, and between man and man. His life and death became a perfect sermon concerning how man could obtain peace with the Father in Heaven and with his fellow man.

Jesus not only lived a good life and taught man how to attain it, but he also died on Cavalry to make it available to all.

Whether by night or day, from mountainside or boat, at a dinner table or on the street, from a well curb or hanging on the cross, Jesus spoke to man the gracious words of life. He spoke as one of authority. He confirmed his words through endless miracles. What man ought to know about God and living with others, about life and salvation, he can come to know through Christ Jesus.

My friends, today in this dark, troubled and confused world, the Lord Jesus continues to speak the gracious words of life. How we should yearn and love to listen to His message.

Are you confused about life? Are you living in darkness? Is your life flooded with countless anxieties?

Moses said, "The Lord your God will raise up for you, a prophet like me. Hear His words. Listen and obey."

Prayer:

Almighty God, help us see Jesus as the One of whom Moses and the prophets of old foretold. Rule and govern our minds by Your Holy Spirit, that we become vividly aware that He and He alone is our only Consolation and Hope, Redeemer and Savior, Lord and Master, Refuge and Destroyer of enemies. Lift up our souls that we eagerly make ready a place for Him in our hearts; so He can remove the confusion and doubt, darkness and despair within our lives. We pray these things in the name of Him whom You have sent to us, so that whosoever believe in Him might not perish, but have eternal life. AMEN

(For the continuation of this Prayer, see "PRAYER" on page 2 in the Suggestions segment)

Hymn: "Joy to the World, the Lord has Come"

A Time of Hope

Hymn: "O Savior, Precious Savior"

Scripture Lesson: Luke 1:67-79

Sermon: "A Time of Hope"

During these days before Christmas, you should be experiencing Christian adventure. You should be undergoing a new spiritual lease on life, and reinvigoration. For a spirit of expectancy and enthusiasm comes to all who truly remember the hope that God brings to man through the Lord Jesus Christ.

As stated in the 15th chapter of Romans, verse 13: "May the God of Hope fill you with joy and peace. By the power of the Holy Spirit, may your whole life and outlook become radiant with hope."

To hope means to desire with the expectation of obtaining what is desired. Hope means believing that the desire will be fulfilled.

It is true that darkness hovers over and around us, and that many of our so-called noble visions of the past have become blurred. It's true that life can be likened unto a small ship caught at sea in the midst of a violent storm. Life can toss us helplessly to and fro.

But it is also true that if the Holy Spirit dwells within our hearts and souls, we are made aware of the fact that there are mightier forces at work than the forces of this world. The Holy Spirit enables us to become aware of the existence of the Almighty God and Creator, aware that God is the Loving Father in Heaven, and aware that He is a Father of Goodness and Mercy. In other words, in spite of the burdens and anxieties you and I encounter, as the result of the Holy Spirit working within us, we are given hope.

And this hope can play a vital role in relation to the individual's outlook on life. That is to say, if one nourishes this hope, one is bound to reap peace and joy. On the other hand, if one shuts out this hope, one is most certainly bound to be caught in the clutches of despair.

These days before Christmas are most certainly a time the Christian ought to be flooded with this hope. For during this time, in a special way, we look beyond what we can do for ourselves. We look beyond what man can do for man. We prepare ourselves for what the Father in Heaven does for humanity through Jesus Christ, the Lord and Savior.

This is what the Apostle Paul implies in our text when he says, "May the God of Hope fill you with joy and peace. By the power of the Holy Spirit, may your whole life and outlook become radiant with hope."

Is your whole life and outlook radiant with the hope that God brings to man through Christ Jesus? Are you permitting the Holy Spirit to dwell within your heart as you make your preparations for Christmas?

If you do possess the hope that something very wonderful and glorious is going to happen, then by all means, reflect this hope. Live your life as if you are in possession of this hope.

In a monthly church magazine, there appeared a cartoon which revealed a great truth concerning the attitude of many this time of year. A husband and wife were standing in a candy and soda shop, next to a card rack. The husband had his hands in his pockets, patiently waiting for his wife. The wife held an open card in her hand. With an annoyed expression upon her face, she was speaking to her husband. The caption read, "There are so many religious cards these days — they are just ruining Christmas."

I wonder what Christmas meant to this woman. One quick glance at the cartoon indicated that her life and outlook were certainly not radiant with hope.

We need not follow the herd simply because others have made this season a commercial venture. At this time of year, you and I, as fellow believers, have a tremendous responsibility — a responsibility not only to ourselves, but to others as well.

In order to fulfill this responsibility, we dare not decorate the interiors and exteriors of our rooms with manger scenes, angels, stars, wreaths, and trees, simply because others do. Rather, we must decorate our surroundings with two and only two purposes in mind. First, that these decorations might strengthen the hope which we already possess. Secondly, that they might instill hope in others.

Remember, sending a Christmas card with Santa's picture on the front only reflects that we have hope in Santa — whereas a Christmas card with a scene pertaining to what happened on the first Christmas Day reflects our hope that God will hear our prayers. Let us have hope that He will provide us with the light for which we so urgently yearn, and which we so desperately need.

My friends, "May the God of Hope fill you with joy and peace in your believing. By the power of the Holy Spirit, may your whole life and outlook become radiant with hope."

<u>Prayer</u>:

Merciful and loving Father in Heaven, may the coming of the Shepherd you have sent enable us to conquer our burdens and afflictions. May this Savior transform and restore us. Only He can calm the troubled sea of this present life. Only through Him can we penetrate the darkness which hovers over and around us. May the hope we have in the coming of Christ Jesus fill our hearts with peace and joy. And by the power of the Holy Spirit, may our lives radiate this hope. AMEN

(For the continuation of this Prayer, see "PRAYER" on page 2 in the Suggestions segment)

<u>Hymn</u>: "What a Friend We Have in Jesus"

The Perfect Christmas Gift

Hymn: "O Little Town of Bethlehem"

Scripture Lesson: Matthew 1:18 – 2:12

Sermon: "The Perfect Christmas Gift"

By this time, a few of you might have opened some of your Christmas gifts. Others will open their Christmas gifts very soon.

A Christmas gift should accomplish a two-fold purpose. First, it ought to reflect the affection of the giver. Second, it ought to fulfill a need of the receiver.

In the 4th Chapter of John, verse 9, we are told, "God is Love. The greatest demonstration of His Love is revealed in Jesus Christ. God gave us His only begotten Son to fulfill our needs."

For a moment, let us direct our attention to the needs of all humanity. Let us take a good look at the world to which you and I belong. What do we see?

We see trial and tribulation, misery and grief, affliction and perplexity. We see malice, hatred, prejudice, and injustice. We see men being segregated and treated as second-class citizens. We see nations full of fear — trembling men, women, and children. We see human beings walking aimlessly, individuals hopelessly adrift. We see all of this and much more!

We are all failures and criminals, but God does not shout or jeer at us. Despite our constant rebellion against Him — our involvement in the vicious circle of sin — God gives us His Love.

In the midst of our helplessness and hopelessness, God shows us He really cares. "The Word was made Flesh and dwelt among us." In the person of Jesus Christ, God came down from heaven, because He was so deeply moved by our frailties.

Jesus came to give Light to a dark and troubled world. He came to save a condemned and dying people. Will you allow His Coming to be in vain?

Jesus Christ is your only Hope — my only Hope — mankind's only Hope. In Him, we have the prescription for good-will among all men. In Him, we have the prescription for peace: peace of mind, peace of body, peace of soul.

My friends, Jesus Christ has been born.

Behold the Gift, which fulfills our every need. Behold the "Perfect Christmas Gift," Jesus Christ has been born. A wondrous and glorious day has dawned.

GLORY TO GOD IN THE HIGHEST.

PEACE ON EARTH TO YOU – TO ALL MEN.

Prayer: Almighty God, our Creator and Sustainer, we thank You for Your "Gift" of gifts. You did so love the world; You have given us Your only begotten Son. Out of the blackness of the night, a Savior has been born. With Him came peace and hope and healing for everyone. He came to bring us The Way and Truth, Life and Immortality. He came that sinful lives might be changed; that hard hearts might be softened; that dark lives might be illuminated; that the fears of the lonely and sorrowful might be overcome; that the burden of the worn and weary might be lifted; that the gloom and sadness of the broken-hearted might be driven out. He came to answer our every need.

Heavenly Father, we beseech You, fill our hearts with Your Holy Spirit so the coming of Jesus may not be in vain. Grant that we hear His voice as He bids us to come to Him, and that we approach Him with believing hearts. Grant that we approach Him with our problems and heartaches; our anxieties and afflictions; our shortcomings and failures; our tired and heavy, laden bodies. Grant that His birth may truly cheer our hearts. AMEN

(For the continuation of this Prayer, see "PRAYER" on page 2 in the Suggestions segment)

Hymn: "O Come, All Ye Faithful"

The Time is Short

Hymn: "When the Roll Is Called Up Yonder"

Scripture Lesson: Matthew 25:1-13

Sermon: "The Time is Short"

One of the greatest gifts God has given us is our time. And yet, we squander this gift. We misuse this gift. We take this gift for granted.

How foolish we are! I ask you; does it seem possible that the last year has come and gone? We now stand on the threshold of another year. Time moves at a rapid pace; it moves swiftly. Days fly by. Years pass quickly.

In the seventh chapter of his first letter to the Corinthians, Paul tells us: "The time is short."

The Apostle is sincerely concerned as to how we use our time. The Lord God has created us to devote ourselves to His way, not ours. Are we?

We will not live in this world forever. Our time grows shorter and shorter. It is constantly ticking away. It waits for no man. There is no way we can stop it.

Does the year you have just completed, speak well of your relationship with God and your fellow man? Are you satisfied with your habits of worship and prayer and Bible reading? Are you satisfied with the way you have used your talents and resources? I fear, on far too many occasions, we all misuse the time God has given us.

Thank God He has given us another year! Let us use this time more wisely. Hear the words of Saint Paul, "The time is short." My friends, let us begin this New Year by seeking forgiveness for the countless ways we have abused our time in the past.

Let us then resolve to live as God's children, in God's service, to God's glory. Let us resolve to devote more of our precious time to nourishing a new life in Him — through whom we can have eternal life.

During this New Year, let us walk daily hand-in-hand with Jesus.

Prayer:

Dear Lord our God, another year has passed us by. Our journey through the wilderness grows shorter. It has been a year of your abundant blessings toward us and our love ones. We humbly thank You for Your love and goodness. It has also been a year which has known our sins — our rebellion against Your will for us. For these we grieve and implore Your forgiveness. You have given us another year. We thank you for this time. Help us remember the words of St. Paul.

"The time is short."

The Promised Land becomes nearer. We know neither the day nor the hour. Give us your Holy Spirit. Help us to be more watchful. Help us to daily seek forgiveness for the endless ways we have abused our time in the past. Help us during this New Year to daily walk hand-in-hand with Jesus. Through Him, strengthen our relationship with You. AMEN

(For the continuation of this Prayer, see "PRAYER" on page 2 in the Suggestions segment)

Hymn: "Sweet By and By"

A Dream Come True

Hymn: "Hark! The Herald Angels Sing"

Scripture Lesson: Hebrews 2: 14-18

Sermon: "A Dream Come True"

We all have a special dream that we yearn to have fulfilled before we depart to the life after this one. So it was for the man called Simeon, mentioned in the second chapter of Saint Luke's Gospel.

Who was Simeon? By our standards, he was not a man of prominence. He was a simple old man who knew he had little time left.

But Simeon was a man of devout faith. He was a man who deeply loved the Lord God. His faith made him a man of great character. Wherever he went, he seemed to carry with him the Presence of God. Those who knew him believed the Spirit of God lived within him.

As were all the faithful children of God, Simeon had been waiting for the Promised Messiah. He had been waiting for deliverance from the oppressors.

It was Simeon's prayer — his hope, his wish, his dream — that his eyes would see the Deliverer and Savior.

Simeon visited the Temple regularly. One day he was inspired to enter the Temple at a particular time. He saw a young man and woman, also of humble rank, holding a baby. The moment Simeon's eyes fell upon the Infant, the Spirit of God revealed unto him that this Child was the Christ, who he had yearned to see. Simeon asked permission to hold the Infant. He took the Child into his withered arms.

Death now seemed near for Simeon. His prayer had been answered; his dream fulfilled. He experienced a joy beyond human expression. He raised his wet eyes toward Heaven and uttered prophetic words which have, and will, interpret for all ages the significance of the birth of Jesus Christ.

He uttered the familiar words known to us as the Nunc Dimittis:

> "Lord, now lettest Thou Thy servant depart in peace; according to Thy Word. For mine eyes have seen Thy salvation, which Thou hast prepared before the face of all people. A Light to lighten the Gentiles and the Glory of Thy people Israel."

Simeon then returned the Child to His mother and revealed unto Mary the destiny of her Son.

He told Mary that her Son was destined to make many fall and rise. Jesus had been born to change the ways of men. He would set up standards of right and wrong which would offend and outrage, because they would compel men to reshape their values of life.

Simeon's prophecy was fulfilled. Many did fall because of Jesus. Did not the Scribes and Pharisees, the Pilates and Herods, oppose Him? And many did rise. Did not the dishonest custom officials, prostitutes, and the hardened criminals open their ears to Him? This prophecy continues to be fulfilled in our world today.

Simeon also told Mary that her soul would be pierced by a sword because of her Son. Again, his prophecy was fulfilled. Did not Mary see Jesus despised and rejected? Did she not see Him weary from His labors for others and, at the same time, treated with ingratitude and contempt? Did she not see Him subjected to the death of a common criminal, upon a cross?

My friends, likened unto Simeon, you and I have also been blessed. We have seen the birth of Jesus Christ. We have seen God's answer to our endless needs.

Jesus Christ has been born. What does His birth mean to you?

Does your faith in Him allow you to see Him as Simeon did? Do you see Jesus Christ as the answer to your prayers; as the Light which overcomes your darkness; as your Savior and Deliverer?

Or, do your doubts cause you to disbelieve? Does your unwillingness to follow and obey cause you to continue in your ways? Does your love for 'self' and the 'things of this world' cause you to disagree and reject? Will your lack of faith in Him cause you to fall?

Prayer: Lord God, we laud and magnify Your glorious Name for the Gift of Your Son. We joyfully thank You for the countless blessings which He had brought unto us. Fill us with Your Holy Spirit, so we are able to see Him as did Simeon. Grant that we see Him as our Savior — as the answer to our prayers, as the Light which will overcome our darkness, as the One who will deliver us from our oppressors. May the promises He gives to those who believe in Him, drive away the shadows of our despair and heal our human woes. Keep us steadfast in following Him, so we may come safely to Thy heavenly home. AMEN

(For the continuation of this prayer, see "PRAYER" on page 2 in the Suggestions segment)

Hymn: "It Came Upon the Midnight Clear"

Our Needs Transformed

Hymn: "All Hail the Power of Jesus' Name"

Scripture Lesson: John 2: 1-11

Sermon: "Our Needs Transformed"

Jesus had been invited to a wedding reception. The supply of wine became exhausted. This created an anxious situation. The family could not afford to buy extra wine, because they had already exceeded their budget.

Mary turned to Jesus and said, "My Son, they have no more wine." Jesus replied, "Is that your concern or Mine? My time has not yet come."

Mary instructed the servants to do whatever her son commanded. She knew Jesus would solve the problem. But He would do so in His own way and time.

Jesus commanded six large jars be filled to the brim with water. He then transformed the water into wine. Hence, Jesus had performed His first miracle in a small town in Galilee.

The miracle at Cana gave mankind a vision of what was to come. Jesus demonstrated His power, and His new disciples believed in Him. The curtain had been raised. The drama of God, made flesh in Jesus Christ, began to unfold.

The miracle at Cana, as do all His miracles, paints a vivid picture of how Jesus enters the lives of men to overcome the anxieties they encounter, especially when He is invited.

The miracles of Jesus reveal His love and mercy. They fulfill a need. His miracles are not for the purpose of exhibition. A doctor practices medicine because he is a doctor, not to convince the world that he is a doctor. The same is true of Jesus. He performs miracles because He is the Savior of men, not to convince the world He is the Savior.

Someone once remarked to me, "Miracles are a thing of the past." This is not true. Miracles are a manifestation of the power and love of Jesus Christ, which are silently at work everywhere — every hour of every day. Miracles are signs that the Loving Father in Heaven is constantly working within the arena of human history.

The omnipotence of Jesus, which transformed the water into wine, is the same omnipotence that will relieve our spiritual and temporal misery. Jesus Christ has power over all things. He has revealed this power on endless occasions. All He has to do is speak, and it will be done. Our faith must rest upon Christ Jesus, knowing He will use His omnipotence — His power — to overcome our needs.

Martin Luther has said:

> "Speak but a word, mighty Savior and I shall be helped.
>
> My soul is cast down; yet, speak but a word and I shall be relieved.
>
> Care and unrest disturb my heart; yet, speak but a word and my heart shall find peace.
>
> The wine of joy — of trust in Thee is lacking in me and I can only shed streams of water in tears; yet, speak but a word — and pitcher full of comfort and refreshment will be given me.
>
> My heart is still as hard as a stone; yet speak but a word — and it shall become tender and melt.
>
> I now have none of the grace of prayerfulness, and feel myself like a dumb man who cannot utter a word; yet, speak but a word — and the bonds of my tongue will be unloosed, so that I will be able to cry "Abba, Father."
>
> So, too, in regard to temporal wants.
>
> I and my wife and children have not bread — have not the things needful for this life; yet, speak but a word – and the windows of Heaven shall open, and Thy blessing descend.

For Thou art able to do this.

Thou has the power.

It will cost Thee nothing but a word — a sign — a movement of Thine Almighty Will.

Thus is the omnipotence of Jesus a stoop — a stoop upon which faith can lead. "

My friends, whatever your need, take it to the Lord in prayer.

He will shower your needy lives with rich and nourishing blessings. Perhaps He may not always do this in the manner you want Him to. But be assured, He will never deny your need. He will supply your needs in His own way and in His own time. After you tell Him your need, be content to wait in faith for the hour He has appointed.

Remember the words of Isaiah: "Fear not, only believe, and you shall see the Glory of the Lord."

If we believe in Jesus Christ, then as He transformed the water into wine, so will He transform our anxieties into peacefulness; our doubts into trust; our suffering into joy; our death into life.

"Fear not, only believe, and you shall see the Glory of the Lord."

<u>Prayer</u>:

Loving Father in Heaven, You gave Your Son power over all things. Through Him, the needs of countless men and women have been transformed. We are also needy. We pray, therefore, to fill our hearts and souls with Your Holy Spirit. Daily direct us to Jesus. Grant we see Him as our Defense — our Strength — our Hope. We believe — overcome our unbelief and doubts. Help us so to trust Him to find refuge in the shadow of His wings. Through Him, help us fight the good fight, that we may finish the course in the faith. Grant us to fear not, only believe that we may see His Glory. AMEN

(For the continuation of this Prayer, see "PRAYER" on page 2 in the Suggestions segment)

Hymn: "Fight the Good Fight"

How to Live with Suffering

Hymn: "Peace, Perfect Peace"

Scripture Lesson: Revelation 7: 9-17

Sermon: "How to Live with Suffering"

I remember vividly a certain experience I encountered as a boy. An elderly woman approached me with a problem involving her dearest friend. Her friend was bedridden with an incurable disease and was suffering great pain. I was asked, "*Why*? Why must my friend suffer so?"

Being only a boy, I was unable to answer the question. However, as I have pondered this experience throughout the years, I have come to the following conclusion. I was never expected to supply an answer. I was simply being used to help someone openly reflect upon a basic problem.

The same problem troubles many of us. *Why*? Why is there suffering? Why are people burdened with pain, heartache, and anxiety?

As human beings, we all endure some form of suffering. For example, illness always brings a certain amount of pain, even if the difficulty lies in a simple case of indigestion or a headache. Scars on our bodies remind us how we have suffered at various times during the course of our lives. Consider the heartaches you and I have experienced — the fear and worry, the guilt and loneliness, which on numerous occasions tied us in knots.

But who is responsible for this suffering? Is God?

Is it God's fault we do not eat properly or acquire enough sleep? Can we blame Him for not caring for our bodies in the manner we should? Can we hold God responsible for the greed and sinfulness we humans possess? Can we attribute our countless anxieties to Him, when we refuse to listen to His Holy Word?

Can we not say in absolute truthfulness that the majority of our suffering is inflicted upon us either by our own doing, or by our fellow men?

You and I cannot escape the fact; suffering is among the realities of this present life. There is no way we can escape suffering, inasmuch as it is part of the structure of our human existence.

Indeed, as human beings, you and I will have to suffer. Unfortunately, some of us will have to suffer more than others. But this is not to imply that life is not worth living. God the Father has a great plan for us. He sent His Son Jesus Christ into our world so that you and I might share in this glorious plan.

In the 8th chapter of Romans, the Apostle Paul has this to say: "It is plain to anyone with eyes to see, that at the present time, all created life groans in a sort of universal suffering." Paul continues: "However, in my opinion, whatever suffering and pain we may have to go through now is less than nothing compared with the magnificent future God has planned for us. The whole creation is on tiptoes to see the wonderful sight of the sons of God coming into their own. The world of creation cannot as yet see reality, not because it chooses to be blind, but because in God's purpose, it has been so limited. Yet, it has been given hope. And this hope is that in the end, the whole of created life will be rescued from the tyranny of change and decay, and have its share in that magnificent liberty which can only belong to the children of God."

What is Paul saying? Simply, there is a great contrast between the present order in which we are all involved and the new age which will come. The Apostle minimizes our present sufferings in comparison with future glory.

Since we now live in a sinful world, our experience of being God's children, even though it is genuine, is incomplete. When complete, we will enjoy new resurrected bodies which will not be subject to suffering or to corruption. We will embrace a beautiful new universe of light and order. You and I will encounter new life in a completely new world.

The question now confronting us is: How should we live as we wait for this Heavenly future? We must live in the hope given us by Jesus Christ through the work of the Holy Spirit. It is only when we hold fast to this hope that life becomes worth living.

What is life without hope? Hope is connected to desire and anticipation. The joys of today would be greatly marred if we had no hope concerning the future.

Real Christian hope sees the bright side to everything. It prevents discouragement and despondency. It eases pain and suffering. It fills the soul with joy and peace.

Let us always remember that although this present life may not be glory, it is the way to Glory for the believer.

My friends, you cannot escape suffering in this life. Therefore, permit Christ Jesus to become the eternal sunlight which breaks through the thick mists of time. Let Him reveal to you the Truth about the magnificent future planned for those who love Him. Let Him show you the Way.

Prayer: Eternal Father, under the guidance of Your Holy Spirit, constantly direct us to Your Son, Jesus Christ, whom You have sent into our world so we might be made partakers of a glorious Eternal Future. Grant us Your Grace, so we may know beyond all doubt that the sufferings we may now endure, are not worth comparing with the Glory which awaits those who believe in Him. Vouchsafe unto us such an abiding sense of the reality of those things which You have prepared for us through Him, that we rise above our sufferings, heartaches and anxieties. Grant that no clouds of this present life, no impatience or foolish fears or any sufferings of the mind or body, shall break our faith in Him. In time of darkness, give us strength and courage. Make us patient and humble. Enable the hope we have in Christ Jesus to saturate every fiber of our being, so we may overcome. AMEN

(For the continuation of this Prayer, see "PRAYER" on page 2 in the Suggestions segment)

Hymn: "Abide with Me"

Our Search for Peace

Hymn: "My Faith Looks up to Thee"

Scripture Lesson: Matthew 21: 18-22

Sermon: "Our Search for Peace"

Perhaps one of the biggest problems you and I will encounter has its roots embedded in our lack of faith. We yearn to have peace — peace from the manifold perils, the countless tribulations, and the endless trials we encounter in this world.

And the reason we do not always experience this peace can be traced to the difficulty we have in remembering that the grace of our Father in Heaven is sufficient for us. His grace knows neither exhaustion nor limit. Yet, we simply do not drink as deeply as we can.

Peace is a state of tranquility. It is freedom from the devils of anxiety, the worries that torture the mind, the fears and guilt that affect our sleep and body, and the hostilities that possess our souls.

Luscious fruits of peace are growing on the spiritual tree which God has planted. Yet, many of our lives reveal spiritual leanness, simply because we refuse to partake of this glorious fruit which will refresh our parched natures. We allow murky clouds to darken our lives.

But why? Why live in gloom, when bright skies stretch over our heads? Why dwell in a dungeon, when we can possess freedom?

In the 5th chapter of Romans, verses 1-2, Paul states, "Since we are justified by faith, let us grasp the fact that we have peace — peace with God through our Lord Jesus Christ. Through Christ, we have entered a new relationship of grace, and here we stand, in happy certainty of the glorious things He has prepared for us in the future."

Paul continues, "This does not mean of course, that we only have hope of future joy. With the assistance of the Holy Spirit, we can be full of joy here and now, even in our trials and troubles."

When Paul states, "Since by faith we are justified," what does he imply?

As human beings, we ought to be aware of the fact that we are sinners. As sinners, we stand in opposition to our Creator. Inasmuch as the wages of sin are death, we become lost and condemned creatures. And because we are what we are, we cannot possibly, by way of our own merits, provide a remedy for our situation.

However, we do possess the knowledge that through Jesus Christ there is hope. Did He not come to seek and save all men? But before this hope can become a reality, we must be in possession of more than knowledge. We must possess a heartfelt belief that Jesus is our Savior. Such a conviction consists of an unquestionable trust in His promises, an absolute obedience to His commands, and a devoted love for Him as Lord and Master. This trust, obedience and love make up what we refer to as faith. Faith is a complete submission to the Lord Jesus Christ.

Once this faith has been established through the work of the Holy Spirit, the individual becomes justified. This faith enables the individual to live a new life in Christ Jesus, which in turn creates a new relationship between the Creator and the creature. In other words, our faith in Jesus Christ makes it possible for you and me to become justified in the sight of the Almighty God. The fruits of this justification give us assurance that we stand in God's grace.

Man can attribute many things to God's grace and love. He can attribute his home, family, and church. He can attribute that which sustains his physical, mental, and spiritual well-being; that which aids him in time of temptation; and that which assists him in time of affliction; to this Grace. But above all, the supreme expression of the Heavenly Father's Grace is found in what He undertook to do for us through His Beloved Son, the Lord Jesus Christ.

The Apostle Paul attempts to make us realize that if we are justified in God's sight through our faith in Jesus Christ — that is to say, if we are living the new life in Christ Jesus, aware that our sins are forgiven; that we presently stand in the midst of the Heavenly Father's grace; and that an eternal life awaits us at the end of this world's journey — we ought to possess peace. We should possess the peace of God which passeth all understanding, the peace of God which frees men from the war of the mind and the unrest of the soul.

The peace of which Paul speaks is a by-product. It consists of a great deal more than merely being happy or content. It is the end result of our relationship with God through Jesus Christ. If we do not experience this peace, the difficulty can be traced to our weak Christian convictions and our lack of faith.

Again let us listen to the words of Saint Paul: "Since we are justified by faith, let us grasp the fact that we have peace — peace with God through our Lord Jesus Christ. Through Christ, we have confidently entered a new relationship of grace, and here we stand, in happy certainty of the glorious things He has prepared for us in the future. This does not mean that we only have hope of future joys. With the assistance of the Holy Spirit, we can be full of joy here and now, even in our trials and troubles."

My friends, do you possess peace of mind and soul? Or do murky clouds darken your lives? If so, then perhaps your faith is not rooted as deeply as it should be. How deep can you go with your faith? Inasmuch as the grace of God knows neither exhaustion nor limit, the answer is clear. Drink as deep as you can. Drink as deep as you need to. Exactly how deeply are you drinking?

Prayer: O Loving and Merciful Father, we are so weak and full of fear. We therefore implore You to help us overcome our many doubts. Give us that peace which the world cannot give. Teach us the patience of unanswered prayer. Grant, we beseech You, such a steadfast faith in Christ Jesus that we may always have an abiding trust in Your promises and experience freedom from the tormenting anxieties our hearts and minds so often create. AMEN

(For the continuation of this Prayer, see "PRAYER" on page 2 in the Suggestions segment)

Hymn: "O for a Faith That Will Not Shrink"

Even Now, a Priceless Treasure Can Be Ours

Hymn: "Jesus Call Us O'er the Tumult"

Scripture Lesson: Mark 4:30-32

Sermon: "Even Now, a Priceless Treasure Can Be Ours"

In this materialistic world, isn't it true that we all have hopes of finding some kind of priceless treasure? The mere thought of locating such treasure excites us. We cannot help but dream about what this unexpected wealth could do for us.

But none of us need pass through this life likened unto a gold prospector who never makes a strike. We can all strike it rich. The greatest of all treasures is within our reach.

In the 13th chapter of the Gospel of Saint Matthew, verses 44-46, Jesus tells us how to find the treasure which will sustain our every need.

The Lord Jesus says, "Truly, truly I say unto you that the Kingdom of Heaven is like a treasure buried in a field. The man who found it, buried it again, and for sheer joy went and sold everything he had, and bought the field."

"I also say to you the Kingdom of Heaven can be compared to a merchant looking for precious pearls. One day he found such a pearl. He also went and sold everything he had so he could buy it."

In other words, Jesus tells us that the Kingdom of God is the greatest of all treasures. It is a treasure which does not fade, and one which is rich beyond all comparison. No possession could be greater. It is a pearl which surpasses all pearls. Eye hath not seen, nor ear heard, nor has there ever entered the heart of man, the things which God through Christ has prepared for those who love Him.

Now you and I can only see dimly, but the day will come when we shall truly see how exceedingly rich the grace of God really is.

But even now, through Jesus Christ and His precious Gospel, the Holy Spirit enables us to find peace with God and conscience — to find hope in death and Heaven of Glory — to find clean hearts and renewed minds — to find relief from our wants and necessities — to find sustaining nourishment for our hunger and thirst.

Even now, the Lord Jesus Christ can transform our fearful hearts and troubled minds and burdened souls. He can transform our confused lives into beautiful ones with meaning and purpose.

Indeed, being a "believing Christian" is truly a priceless treasure. But as Jesus states, one does not become such a Christian by accident. This blessed experience must be the result of deliberate determination, intelligent seeking, and faithful enduring.

You must want the treasure of which Jesus speaks so badly that you are willing to part with everything else. You must be willing to sacrifice countless worldly possessions and pleasures. You must knock and ask. You must sacrifice time from your normal routine for the purpose of prayer, meditation, and reading your Bible. You must spend less of yourself upon the things of this world and become more involved in the Kingdom of God.

Only by the rugged and narrow path of sacrifice can any man reach the heights of great attainment.

No man can be saved but he who believes — he who lives in Jesus; he who takes up his cross and, denying himself daily, follows Jesus Who is the Way and Truth and Life.

My friends, if you are willing to pay the price for the treasure of which Jesus speaks, you can now begin to enjoy the endless benefits you shall reap. Through Christ Jesus, renew your relationship with God. Through Him, receive deliverance from your sins, the devil, and death. Through Him, obtain the peace which passeth all human understanding. He is a priceless Pearl.

Prayer:

Almighty and loving God, flood our hearts with Your Holy Spirit so we may continually be directed to Your Son Jesus Christ, and the Kingdom He has established. Make us to see this Kingdom as a priceless treasure and the pearl which surpasses all pearls. Help us to sacrifice whatever is necessary so that even now, amid the trials and tribulations of this present life, we may taste the glorious, sustaining fruits of Your Kingdom, which will enable us to experience the peace You have prepared for those who love and follow the Savior of men. Even now, help us to benefit from the endless blessing we can reap through Him that will transform our fearful hearts, troubled minds, and burdened souls. AMEN

(For the continuation of this prayer, see "PRAYER" on page 2 in the Suggestions segment)

Hymn: "Softly and Tenderly"

The Bare Can Become Green

Hymn: "In the Cross of Christ I Glory"

Scripture Lesson: John 20:30-31 and John 21:24-25

Sermon: "The Bare Can Become Green"

Before a seed can produce its fruit, it must die. It dies in order to create life. But although it dies, as a seed, it is not destroyed. Something happens to it. Its wrappings fall off and its substance is transformed. In other words, once the seed has been sown, it must perish to accomplish its purpose. It must die in order to give life that will produce fruit.

In the 12th chapter of the Gospel of Saint John, Jesus says, "The time has come for the Son of Man to be glorified. Truly, truly, I say unto you, that if a grain of wheat does not fall into the earth and die, it remains a single grain of wheat. But, if the grain of wheat falls into the ground and dies, it brings forth a good harvest. My hour of heartbreak has come. Can I say, 'Father, save Me from this hour?' No, for it was for this purpose that I came. Only if I am lifted up from the earth, can I draw all men to Myself." He said this to show the kind of death He was going to die.

Before Jesus entered this world of ours, man was unproductive and barren. As the result of man's opposition to God, there was no harvest. So that man might produce fruit pleasing to his Father in Heaven, Jesus came to seek and save the lost. He came so that men might have life and be drawn to God for all eternity. But to complete His mission of man's redemption, Jesus — likened unto a grain of wheat which had fallen into the ground — had to die.

Although death is for sinners, Christ Jesus took the sin of the world upon Himself. He willingly drank the contents of the cup the Father in Heaven had given Him. As we are well aware, this cup was filled with sorrow and torture, pain and horror. This cup contained the Cross on Calvary.

Hence, Calvary's Cross unveiled the heart of God. This Cross becomes a wondrous ladder which brings God to man. It enables us to see God experiencing our temptations, feeling our anxieties, sharing our sorrows, and bearing our sins. It vividly conveys unto us that God is no mere spectator looking down upon us from above. He is a loving and merciful, suffering and sympathizing God in the midst of His people.

The Cross of Jesus also becomes a ladder which brings man to God. This Cross is the means by which the Creator welcomes the unclean and lost, the troubled and enslaved. It is the means which permit you and me, through the work of the Holy Spirit, to find our way to the Heavenly Father. This Cross is where God, through Christ Jesus, is willing to take upon His heart the heavy burden of our sins.

Indeed, the passion and death of Jesus Christ is a glorious ladder set up between Heaven and Earth – between you and God.

The Holy Scriptures enables us to better understand the true meaning of the Cross. The Bible presents us with the unique opportunity of being drawn to the Cross of Jesus, and of partaking of the eternal fruit which is ours for the taking.

If permitted, conscientious and faithful reading of the Holy Scriptures will accomplish a great deal for our spiritual well-being. It will help us to comprehend how terrible and horrible the evil forces at work within our lives really are. Sin makes the soul empty and bare. It pierces the hands of God. It drives a spike through innocent feet. It thrusts a spear into the heart of love. Can there be any doubt? Sin is ugly and destructive.

But the Bible also enables us to become better aware of the fact that the full weight of our sins has been placed upon the shoulders of Christ Jesus. He was stricken for our transgressions so that we might be healed. He died so that the bareness and emptiness within our souls might be transformed into greenness and eternal beauty.

In one of the smaller cities in Connecticut, there is a high hill upon which stands a big cross. I have seen similar scenes in other cities. I suppose this is why I personally find the following story so meaningful.

A small boy was crying as if his little heart would break at any moment. "What is wrong?" asked a nearby policeman. The boy replied, "I am lost."

"That is nothing to cry about," said the policeman. "Tell me where you live, and I will help you." The boy said, "If you can direct me to the high hill where the big cross stands, I will be able to find my way home."

My friends, we are all sheep who have gone astray. Therefore, should we not make a more sincere effort to permit the Holy Scriptures to direct us to the Cross of Jesus Christ, so we can also find our way home?

And Jesus said, "The time has come for the Son of Man to be glorified. Truly, truly I say unto you, that if a grain of wheat does not fall into the earth and die, it remains a single grain of wheat. But if the grain of wheat falls into the ground and dies, it brings forth a good harvest. My hour of heartbreak has come. Can I say, 'Father, save Me from this hour?' No, for it was for this purpose that I came."

Prayer: Merciful God and Father, grant us your grace that we may study the Holy Scriptures diligently, and with our hearts and minds, seek and find Your Son; and through Him, obtain whatever we need to sustain our daily necessities.

Lead us by Your Holy Spirit so that we may always have Christ Jesus, Who is the Savior of the world and Shepherd of our souls, before us. Direct us to His Cross and enable us to see His life, passion, and death as our only avenue to eternity with You. AMEN

(For the continuation of this Prayer, see "PRAYER" on page 2 in the Suggestions segment)

Hymn: "When I Survey the Wondrous Cross"

What to Do with Your Temptations

Hymn: "Guide Me, O Thou Great Jehovah"

Scripture Lesson: James 4:7-8a

Sermon: "What to Do with Your Temptations"

Each new day, you and I encounter evil temptations in one form or another. Submission to these temptations makes us oppose our Creator's Will. For our well-being, it is vital that we wage war against these temptations.

But how do we do this? How do we human beings maintain a foothold against Satan?

To answer this question, let us direct our attention to the 4th chapter of the Gospel of Saint Matthew, verses 1-11. Consider how Jesus dealt with His temptations.

Immediately after Jesus was baptized in the river Jordan, He was led into the wilderness by the Spirit. Here for forty days and nights, He meditated and prayed upon His ministry.

Jesus experienced extreme hunger. He had gone without food for days. Satan approached Him, and cunningly whispered in His ear, "Why are you going without food? Use the power which has been entrusted to you. Why be so foolish? Give up these high aspirations. Think more of yourself. Satisfy your own needs. Attain basic comfort. Enjoy life."

But Jesus replied, "Man shall not live by bread alone, but by every word that proceedeth out of the mouth of God."

Then Satan tempted Jesus to put the love of His Heavenly Father to a test. He made Jesus envision He was on the highest ledge of the Temple in Jerusalem. He enticed Jesus to win the adoration of men by jumping. Had the Holy Scriptures not made it clear, "He will give His angels charge over you?"

But Jesus answered, "Thou shall not tempt the Lord your God."

Again, Satan tempted Jesus. If Jesus would only worship him, Satan would give Him all the kingdoms of the world, and the glory of them. Certainly what Satan requested could not be compared to what God demanded. To establish God's Kingdom would demand that Jesus endure trial and hardship, suffering and death. And when God's Kingdom has been established, how many people would truly appreciate what Jesus had done?

Jesus replied, "Be gone, Satan. I shall worship the Lord My God, and Him only shall I serve." And Satan departed.

In all His temptations, Jesus was urged to forsake the course His heavenly Father would have Him follow. If Jesus had in any way surrendered unto Satan, He would have forfeited His chances of being our Savior. He would have taken away all hope for the human race.

If you and I are not to be led astray by Satan, we must follow in the footsteps of Jesus. He conquered His temptations with a quotation from the Holy Scripture. Let us do likewise.

The Father in Heaven has spoken many Words for the sole purpose of giving us guidance in whatever circumstances we may find ourselves. If we spent more time feeding ourselves upon His Word, and then "become doers of this Word," and not hearers only, our self-inflicted anxieties would vanish.

Consider, if when we are tempted to envy or despise — tempted to take advantage of or mistreat others — we said, "I shall love my neighbor as myself."

If when our lives are flooded with apprehension and despair, we said, "Yea, though I walk through the valley of the shadow of death, I will fear no evil. His rod and His staff will comfort me."

If when our souls are filled with the fear of death itself, we said, "Whosoever believeth in Jesus Christ shall never die."

If when we are afflicted with burdens and distress, we said, "I will cast my cares upon the Lord, knowing He will sustain me."

If when we struggle with feelings of guilt, we said, "Jesus has the power to forgive sins. If we confess our sins unto Him, He will forgive us."

If when we are consumed with doubt, we prayed, "Lord, I believe. Help Thou my unbelief."

If when loneliness engulfs us, we said, "I know He will be with me always, even unto the end of this world. He will neither leave me, nor forsake me."

You and I need always remember, the Holy Scriptures were written that "we might believe Jesus Christ is the Son of God and that, in believing, we might have life through Him."

Do you not agree? Our lives would be richly blessed if we human beings answered our temptations as Jesus did — with the Word of God.

However, to do this, you and I must prepare ourselves. As Jesus withdrew into the wilderness to prepare Himself, so must we do the same. We must feed upon the Word of God. We must meditate upon His Word.

We must brush the dust off our Bibles and make them play a vital role in our lives.

The more nourishment we obtain from God's Word, the better equipped we will be to know our path of duty in an instant. No temptation can prevail against us, if we calmly and fairly consider what God tells us to do in whatever predicament we find ourselves. If we resolve to surrender our will to the Heavenly Father's Will, if we are determined to answer our temptations with His Word; Satan will depart from us.

My friends, as recorded in the epistle of James: "Blessed is the man who endures temptations and trials, for after he has stood the test, he will receive the crown of life which the Lord has promised to those who love Him."

<u>Prayer</u>: Father in Heaven — the comfort of the sorrowful, the strength of the weak, and the friend of the tempted — we pray that You protect us with Your grace. Fill us with Your Holy Spirit. Deliver us from whatever temptations we encounter, lest they overcome our hearts and minds. Enable us to follow the example of Christ Jesus. Grant that with Your Holy Scriptures in hand, we watch and pray. Grant that as we walk along life's

road, Your Word may guide and direct us. Make us doers of Your Word, not hearers only. AMEN

(For the continuation of this Prayer, see "PRAYER" on page 2 in the Suggestions segment)

Hymn: "Onward, Christian Soldiers"

Accepting His Message

Hymn: "More Love to Thee"

Scripture Lesson: John 1: 14-18

Sermon: "Accepting His Message"

At the east entrance to Rockefeller Center, an inscription reads, "Man's ultimate destiny depends not on whether he can learn new lessons or make new discoveries and conquests, but on his acceptance of the lesson taught him, close upon two thousand years ago."

How true! The Lord Jesus taught man the Way and the Truth. He revealed what man must do to have a proper relationship with his Creator, and with his fellow man.

But man refuses to heed the teachings of Christ! Today's world witnesses to this fact. An excellent illustration concerning man's reaction to the message of Jesus Christ is found in the 8th chapter of the Gospel of Saint John.

Jesus told His contemporaries why He came into the world. But the more He revealed to them, the less they believed.

Finally, Jesus said, "If God were really your Father, as you claim Him to be, you would love and believe Me. For I have come from God, and I am with you now as One sent from God. I did not come of My own accord — He sent Me. The reason why you do not believe My words is that you cannot bear to hear what I have to say. "

Jesus then challenged His opponents. "Who among you can convict Me of any disobedience to God?" There was no reply. Jesus continued, "On the basis of the validity of this claim that I am without sin, can it not be said therefore, I am the perfect Revealer of the Truth? And, if I do speak the Truth, why is it you will not believe Me? You do not believe My words because you do not want to hear them. And you do not want to hear them because you are not of God."

Needless to say, the words of Jesus had the same effect upon His opponents as does salt in an open wound. They were the religious leaders of Israel. They believed they were above reproach. Who was this Jesus to affront them with such authority? They drove Jesus from their sight.

But why — why did these religious leaders despise and reject the Message of Jesus?

The contemporaries of Jesus were looking for a Messiah who was more devoted to the physical and materialistic life than the spiritual. They were more concerned with an earthly kingdom than a Heavenly one. They were blind. They did not see their need for salvation. They were oblivious to their sin.

Unfortunately, many of us are to be likened unto these religious leaders. On far too many occasions, we also are much more concerned with the physical and materialistic aspects of life than with the spiritual.

Too often, we too are blind to the fact that we are lost and condemned creatures. Therefore, like the religious leaders of Israel, we do not accept the Message of Jesus Christ. This is evident through the sparse effort we make to incorporate His Message into a vital part of our lives.

Some time ago, I spoke with someone who confessed to be a Christian. We discussed sin. Much to my surprise, this individual stated she was not a sinner, because she fulfilled the requirements of the Ten Commandments. I pointed out that, according to the interpretation which Jesus gives to these commandments, all men are sinners. I was informed by this woman that she could not agree with Jesus regarding this matter.

How true this is, of so many of us. As long as Jesus Christ says what we want to hear, we are quick to accept His Message. But when He begins to cramp our style, we want no part of this Message. When we feel He is demanding too much, we shut our eyes, plug our ears, and go merrily on our way.

Who among us has not rebelled against the Words of Jesus? It is this rebellion, which makes the world what it is today!

Jesus Christ is the perfect Revealer of Truth. If we are children of light and not children of darkness, we shall hunger for His Truth. We will crave the food Jesus gives. We will love and listen to His Message, in spite of the demands it places upon us.

In other words, how much you hunger and thirst for the Way and the Truth, determines the role that the Gospel of Christ plays in your life.

My friends, consider the dear price Jesus Christ paid to illuminate the road of life.

Why do so many of us, like the religious leaders of Israel, still travel those roads where there is no light?

Remember: "Your ultimate destiny depends not on whether you can learn new lessons or make new discoveries and conquests, but on your acceptance of the lesson taught, close upon two thousand years ago."

<u>Prayer</u>: Lord God, our Creator and Sustainer, we humbly thank You for the Gift of Your only begotten Son, Jesus Christ. Fill us with Your Holy Spirit. Enable us to see that You have sent Jesus into our world, so we might have life. Enable us to behold Him as the Revealer of the Way and the Truth. Grant that His Message, which is able to save our souls, may become a lamp unto our feet and a light unto our path. Make His Words a vital part of our lives. Let them lead and bring us into Your Holy Hill. AMEN

(For the continuation of this Prayer, see "PRAYER" on page 2 in the Suggestions segment)

<u>Hymn</u>: "Have Thine Own Way, Lord"

Are You Taking Jesus Seriously?

Hymn: "I Think, When I Read That Sweet Story of Old"

Scripture Lesson: John 8:12, Matthew 7:21-28

Sermon: "Are You Taking Jesus Seriously?"

In the 22nd chapter of the Gospel of Saint Matthew, and again in the 12th chapter of the Gospel of Saint Mark, we are told that the Pharisees approached Jesus to test Him. They asked, "Master, what are we to consider the Law's greatest commandment?"

Jesus replied, "Thou shalt love the Lord your God with all your heart, and with all your soul, and with all your mind. This is the first and great commandment. And there is a second like it. Thou shalt love your neighbor as yourself. The whole of the Law and the prophets depends upon these two commandments."

The Pharisees had not expected such a simple answer. They were speechless.

Jesus seized the opportunity to enlighten the Pharisees about the Promised Messiah. They believed the Messiah would come from the line of the great King David. His Kingdom would be of this world. His purpose for coming would be to overthrow the Roman oppressors and institute a prosperous Jewish State.

Jesus knew this misconception prevented many of His contemporaries from accepting Him as the Promised Messiah — from accepting His teachings.

Hoping to overcome this misconception, Jesus asked the Pharisees, "What do you think of the Christ? Whose Son is He?" They replied, "The Son of David." This was the answer Jesus anticipated. Jesus then asked, "How then does David when, inspired by the Spirit, call Him Lord? If David then calls Him Lord, how can He be His son?" In other words, how can the Christ be both the Son and the Lord of David?

Not one was able to answer Jesus. The Pharisees slowly walked away. The Master's Words made no impact. Their opinion of Jesus had not been altered. They still did not take Him seriously. They walked away as if nothing had happened. They walked away as if nothing had to be done.

Are you to be likened unto the Pharisees? "What do you think of the Christ?"

No one need listen to your answer, to know what you think of Jesus. Your answer is revealed by the way you live.

Unfortunately, our lives reveal that we do not take Jesus seriously. After hearing His Words, time and time again we walk away as if nothing had happened. We walk away as if nothing had to be done.

Jesus Christ is the promised Messiah. He is the Savior and Redeemer; High Priest and Mediator; Teacher and Example. He came to reveal the existence and nature of God — the meaning and destiny of life — the goal of human effort. He came to show us how to live. He came to free us from our oppressors. He came to give us endless Grace that we might rise above the power of death.

My friends, "What do you think of the Christ?"

Are you too happy ... too worried ... too busy ... too tired ... too proud ... too indifferent ... too materialistic ... too weak ... too handicapped ... too ill to take him seriously?

One day, it will be too late to take Him seriously!

<u>Prayer</u>: Heavenly Father, we thank You that You sent Your Son unto us, that through Him, we might know You truly, love You purely, and worship You rightly. Grant that we be not likened unto the Scribes and Pharisees, who refused to take Jesus seriously. We believe; help us overcome our unbelief. Let us be newborn babes desiring the milk of His Words. Help us to call upon Him while He is near and seek Him while He may be found. Let Him be the Bread that satisfies our hunger; the Water that quenches our thirst; the Shepherd that cares for our soul; the Door that leads us to Your eternal Heavenly Home. We beseech You, fill us with Your Holy

Spirit so that our ears hear, our hearts receive, our minds understand, and our lives show forth His saving Gospel. AMEN

(For the continuation of this Prayer, see "PRAYER" on page 2 in the Suggestions segment)

Hymn: "O Worship the King"

What Has Happened to Us?

Hymn: "Dear Lord and Father of Mankind"

Scripture Lesson: Genesis 1: 27-31

Sermon: "What Has Happened to Us?"

Several years ago, I had the opportunity to visit an old country church, located in the beautiful hills of upstate New York. This was an experience I would never forget. At one time, this building must have been a very warm and inviting structure. It had been erected for the purpose of worshiping the Lord.

But what at one time had been appealing to the human eye, now stood in contrast with the beauty which surrounded it. The building itself had become weather-beaten. Ugly weeds had taken the place of beautiful grass.

I entered the building, only to discover darkness. All the windows had been boarded up. However, enough light passed through the opening from the door to enable me to see what the interior looked like.

What I saw was heartbreaking. Dirt covered the broken pews and torn hymnals. The pulpit had been destroyed. The altar had been removed.

Upon leaving the building, I found it difficult convincing myself that, years ago, people had actually assembled here to worship the Loving Father in Heaven.

Meeting a nearby native, I inquired if the old church had been used recently for any special reason. I was informed it had been used to make "potato-jack." I asked, "What is potato-jack?"

"It is an illegal booze with a tremendous kick," was the reply.

Incredible, isn't it? What at one time had been a lovely structure, had become a home of darkness and dirt surrounded by weeds. What at one time had been a House of Worship, had become a den of iniquity and thieves.

That little old church building in upstate New York is the story of mankind. Our Creator created us to be His — to be structures of beauty and houses of worship. What has happened to us?

Let us take a good look at ourselves to see what we have really become. While we still have the opportunity, let us take time from the hustle and bustle of everyday life to do something about our relationship with God.

Prayer: Lord God and Father of Love, You have created us in Your Image — to be creatures of beauty and structures of worship. What has happened to us? We have become creatures of the world and of darkness. We honor You with our lips, but on far too many occasions, our hearts are far from You.

Likened unto the Apostle Paul, we do those things we should not do. And do not do the things we should. Lord, have mercy upon us. Forgive us! Send us the Holy Spirit. Help us see what we have become. Help us do something about our sin and our relationship with You. Each new day, direct us to Jesus, who is the Way, the Truth, and the Life. Help us overcome and be what you created us to be. AMEN

(For the continuation of this Prayer, see "PRAYER" on page 2 in the Suggestions segment)

Hymn: "Just as I Am, Without One Plea"

The Advantage of Wings

Hymn: "Dear Lord and Father of Mankind"

Scripture Lesson: Isaiah 40: 28-31

Sermon: "The Advantage of Wings"

Did you know that a certain species of ant are born with wings? However, rather than using their wings to fly, for some strange reason these ants tear them from their bodies and remain crawling insects.

Likened unto these ants, we also have the opportunity to raise ourselves upward. Yet, on endless occasions, we crawl.

In the 40th chapter of Isaiah, verse 31, we are told:

> "They who wait for the Lord shall renew their strength,
>
> They shall mount up with wings like eagles,
>
> They shall run and not be weary,
>
> They shall walk and not faint."

The prophet Isaiah speaks to a people who had been uprooted and torn away from their native soil. Freedom for the Israelites had become nothing more than an optimistic dream. In addition to the tribulations caused by their exile, the world was in a dubious state. Empire was against empire. The earth rocked beneath the clashes between nations.

The Israelites had grown discouraged and weary. They wondered what would be next.

The countless trials confronting Israel had become physical, mental, and spiritual parasites, feeding upon the Israelites' energy and vitality. The long, grim years of captivity and the tide of world events had taken their toll.

In an effort to overcome the oppression which weighed heavily upon the hearts of the Israelites, the prophet Isaiah spoke.

To Isaiah, it was evident that the people of Israel had forgotten the many ways in which the Lord God had revealed His love and concern for them. There had been nothing in the world mightier than the Empire of Pharaoh. At the same time, there was nothing in the world weaker than the baby Moses, who cried in his handmade crib by the banks of the Nile River. But in God's Plan, that helpless baby was used to rend the might of Egypt and set the Israelites free. Had the people of Israel forgotten what the Lord their God was capable of doing?

Isaiah reminded his people that the Lord God is all-powerful and everlasting. The enemies of righteousness may win many battles, but in the long run, God will win the war. Their faith should not be deceived by unfortunate circumstance.

The prophet informed his people that more than ever before, they needed the Lord God, who is the means of all-sustaining power. They must, therefore, trust in Him. They must wait for Him, and in their waiting, they would find new strength.

The situation which confronted Israel hundreds of years ago does not differ very much from the one which confronts many of us today. We endure the same physical, mental, and spiritual fatigue. We suffer the same discouragements and frustrations, disheartenment and despondency. We encounter the same weariness. Like the Israelites, we are also imprisoned by our own physical problems, as well as by public and worldly affairs.

We cannot help but wonder what will be next.

As human beings, we need strength. We need strength to cope with any one of the hundreds of problems that come our way during the course of a single day. Our own strength will not suffice. We need Divine strength.

Likened unto the Israelites, many of us have forgotten the many ways in which God the Father has revealed His love and concern for us.

There was nothing in the world mightier than the Empire of Rome. At the same time, there was nothing weaker than the Baby lying in a manger in Bethlehem. Yet, from that weak and helpless Baby, came a Power which laid the mightiest empire of ancient times to dust.

On Good Friday, there appeared to be nothing in the world mightier than the devil, sin, and death. At the same time, nothing seemed weaker than a man called Jesus who had died upon a Cross. Yet it was God's plan that three days later, this dead Jesus would conquer the power of the grave and set us free.

If you and I follow the advice of the prophet Isaiah, we will not become weary. He tells us that, "Those who wait for the Lord shall renew their strength." The key word is *wait*.

Whatever your trial or tribulation is; *wait*. Wait, trusting and believing that God will act according to His will in due time. First we knock, and then we wait for the door to open. While the knocking may only require a moment, the waiting may be long. But wait — wait with an air of expectancy, knowing that sooner or later, the door will open.

My friends, be assured that God the Father will not fail us. He who believes this Truth will have his strength renewed. And with renewed strength, you will mount up with wings like an eagle. You will rise up above the pressures of the earth — above the ups and downs of this human life. In flight, the eagle has purer air and clearer vision, peace and unclouded skies.

> "Truly, if you wait for the Lord, you shall renew your strength.
>
> You shall mount up with wings like an eagle.
>
> You shall run and not be weary.
>
> You shall walk and not faint."

Prayer:

O God, the refuge of the needy and the strength of the weak, let not our faith in You be deceived by the trials and tribulations we encounter in this life. Flood our hearts and minds with Your Holy Spirit, so we might have continued assurance You will not fail us. Strengthen us by Your grace, so that like eagles, we can rise above the dark clouds which hover over us. Give us patience, knowing in due time, You will restore and relieve us from the perils which assail us. Direct us to Your Son, Jesus Christ, and His redeeming love. Remind us of the endless blessings which You have prepared through Him, for those who trust You. Remind us that through Him, You are able to sustain our every need. AMEN

(For the continuation of this Prayer, see "PRAYER" on page 2 in the Suggestions segment)

Hymn: "This is My Father's World"

The End That Never Comes

Hymn: "The Day of Resurrection"

Scripture Lesson: 1 Corinthians 15: 50-57

Sermon: "The End that Never Comes"

The Gospel of Saint Matthew tells us that, "Peter sat down and waited for the end."

"Peter sat down and waited for *the end*."

Jesus had informed Peter, along with the others, that He would endure bitter suffering and death, but would rise on the third day. But Peter and his companions were unable to grasp the significance of what Jesus had said. The big fisherman revealed his lack of understanding in the Garden of Gethsemane, when he drew his sword.

However, Peter did understand that the hatred which the religious leaders possessed for Jesus, had reached its climax. When the Temple guards and Roman soldiers seized Jesus, Peter feared the worst. As Jesus was being taken to the Sanhedrin, the Supreme Court of Israel, Peter followed at a safe distance. While the mock trial was in session, "Peter sat down and waited for the end."

Peter did not have long to wait. Within a few short hours, Jesus had been crucified like a common criminal on a hill called Calvary, outside the walls of Jerusalem. Jesus was dead.

To Peter and the others, death was so final. Therefore, their lives were flooded with emptiness, darkness, and hopelessness. Their hearts were burdened with grief and sorrow. Their minds were tortured by despair and loneliness.

Jesus was gone. Jesus was gone forever. Now, all that could be done was to remove His lifeless Body from the Cross and give it a proper and decent burial. The Body was placed in a dark, cold tomb. The entrance was sealed with a large stone. Hence, Jesus Christ has been "crucified, dead and buried."

But the blackness of night always comes before the light of the day.

The end which Peter had anticipated, never really came. On the morning of the third day, the tomb was empty. Had this been the result of grave robbers? Indeed not. It had been the Work of the Almighty God. The Lord Jesus Christ had risen from the dead. The Son of God had burst forth from the grave to bring a glorious new dawn to all mankind.

The darkness which had filled the lives of Peter and his companions now began to give way to a wondrous and beautiful light. The pieces of the puzzle began to fit together.

The followers of Jesus began to understand that His death was not the end, but rather the beginning. His death became the gateway to victory over the grave.

Sin can no longer condemn us. Jesus has destroyed the poisonous fangs. "O Death, where is thy sting?"

Jesus Christ lives! And, because He lives, you and I can also live. Jesus says, "I am the Vine. If you believe in Me, love Me, trust and obey Me, follow and serve Me, you shall be My branches." If the Vine lives, surely the branches will live also.

Life for the believer is not a dead-end street. The door at the end of the hallway of life will always be open. "The grave itself has become nothing more than a tunnel, leading from light to light through a brief darkness."

For the believer, death can now become life's finest form of adventure. It is simply the changing of homes. It is like watching a ship go out to sea. When the ship departs, you say, "There she goes." But on the other side of the sea, when the ship is sighted, someone says, "Here she comes."

When death calls the believer, someone on earth will say, "There he goes." But at the same time, someone in Heaven will say, "Here he comes."

Hear the Words of Jesus:

"Do not let your hearts be troubled. In my Father's House there are many mansions. I go to prepare a place for you."

"I am the Way and the Truth — the Resurrection and the Life. He that believeth in Me, though he were dead, yet, shall he live. And whosoever liveth and believeth in Me, shall never die."

My friends, let us not be compared to Peter before the Resurrection. He saw death as *"the end."* His life, therefore, was flooded with emptiness, darkness, and hopelessness. His heart was burdened with grief and sorrow. His mind was tortured by despair and loneliness.

How differently Peter viewed death after the Resurrection of Jesus Christ.

May God the Father grant that the Resurrection of Christ Jesus will do for you, what it did for Peter.

<u>Prayer</u>:

Almighty God, author and giver of Life, Who has given us Your Son, Christ Jesus, that in Him we might have the life which knows no end. Give us such an abiding faith in Him, that we overcome all fear of death. Give us the assurance that He has prepared a place in Your Eternal Mansion for all who love and trust and follow Him. Grant that we find peace and joy in the blessed hope of the resurrection of the dead, and the Glory of the World to come.

Fill us with Your Holy Spirit, so we may have confidence that the door at the end of the hallway of this present life will always be open. Grant us the certainty that death is merely a change of homes, a tunnel of brief darkness leading from this life of sorrow and pain to a Glorious Eternal Life with You. Enable us at all times to commend our hearts and souls, minds and bodies unto You through our Lord and Savior, Jesus Christ. AMEN

(For the continuation of this Prayer, see "PRAYER" on page 2 in the Suggestions segment)

<u>Hymn</u>: "I Know that My Redeemer Lives"

Why Live in The Valley of Hopelessness?

Hymn: "Come, Ye Faithful, Raise the Strain"

Scripture Lesson: John 20: 1-18

Sermon: "Why Live in the Valley of Hopelessness?"

Mary Magdalene was one of the women who discovered the empty tomb on that Easter Sunday morning of long ago. Mary Magdalene was the first person to whom Jesus Christ appeared after His resurrection.

How her face must have glowed upon becoming aware of the fact that the Lord had risen from the dead. Upon hearing His Voice, her feelings of hopelessness vanished — her troubled spirit was transformed into a peaceful and joyful soul.

Who was this Mary Magdalene? Mary had come from Magdala, a small village located west of the Sea of Galilee. She had been possessed by the powerful influence of the devil. She had become a helpless and hopeless human being, living in profound misery. It was while she was slowly disintegrating that Jesus found her. He restored her and set her free from her oppressor.

Mary could not forget what Jesus had done for her, nor could she cease being grateful. She therefore devoted her heart and energies to her Lord's ministry. For example, we can be sure the purse that Judas carried was supplied in part by Mary.

Whenever possible, Mary followed Jesus on His preaching missions. Knowing her weaknesses, she knew how vital it was to depend upon the Master for the strength which would enable her to continue the life to which she had been called. Indeed, Mary needed Jesus more than mere words can convey. That is why she was always near Him.

Mary had witnessed the crucifixion. She had seen her Lord die. She had been present when His Body was removed from the Cross and carried to the tomb in the garden belonging to Joseph of Arimathea. She had watched the men place the heavy stone over the mouth of this tomb.

And then, filled with grief, she returned to her home, because it was the Sabbath.

As she observed the Sabbath Day, excruciating anxieties flooded Mary's soul. What would happen to her? Jesus was dead and buried. And to make matters worse, the devil was launching an all-out attack against her in an effort to once again gain possession of her life. Mary trembled as she recalled the horror of her past.

After experiencing an endless night, Mary joined the other women early Sunday morning. Together, they made their way to the tomb to anoint the Lord's Body. This was to be their last tribute of love to Jesus.

But upon reaching the tomb, much to their amazement, they discovered that the large stone covering the door of the tomb had already been rolled away. The tomb was empty. The women quickly left the garden to inform Peter and John of their discovery. After investigating the situation, the two disciples departed.

Alone, Mary returned to the tomb. She was thrown into the pit of sorrow and the valley of hopelessness. Her eyes, already red from weeping, shed even more tears. Her Beloved Master was not only dead, but now His Body had mysteriously disappeared.

Then, Mary heard a familiar Voice: "Woman, why are you weeping? Why are you so troubled?" The Voice even called her by name. She had heard this Voice speak her name on countless occasions. Mary turned and saw the Risen Lord. She said, "Oh Master — You live." Her feeling of hopelessness suddenly vanished. His Voice had transformed her troubled spirit into a peaceful and joyful soul.

May the Resurrection of Jesus Christ do for us what it did for Mary Magdalene.

Jesus lives. He has overcome the world. He has conquered the grave. He has won a decisive victory over the power of the devil and sin. And we have His pledge and promise that because He lived, we who live in Him shall also live.

It is true, the world may tug us in this direction and that direction as it did with Mary Magdalene. This world may be cruel and harsh. Our bodies may hurt from the wounds we carry. Our minds may be torn with all kinds of anxieties. Our soul may be heavy from the burden of sin. But, as for Mary Magdalene, the Voice of the Risen Lord can transform our troubled spirits into lives which reflect peace and joy.

The Risen Lord is constantly speaking to us in prayer, in meditation, and in the Holy Scriptures. And it is important that we listen to and believe this Voice. For if you and I lack the necessary faith — if we possess doubts — we will despair instead of conquer. We will live a life of self-inflicted misery. We will encounter the hell of torment in the darkness of night. And the devil will most certainly have his way.

My friends, *Jesus lives*. And He bids us to live with Him — today, tomorrow and forever more. He is alive to every prayer; to every need; to every broken heart.

The Son of God, who was dead, is gloriously alive. He lives to grant you daily breath. He lives, which means you can conquer death. He lives, your mansion to prepare. He lives, to guide you safely there.

Therefore, why are you troubled? Why live in a valley of hopelessness? The stone has been rolled away. The tomb is empty. The storm is over. The black clouds have disappeared. *Jesus Christ lives! Alleluia!*

<u>Prayer</u>:

O Lord God our Father, we give You heartfelt praise for the joy that floods our hearts and souls for the Resurrection of Jesus. Through His Resurrection, You have bestowed a wondrous hope upon all men. Enable us to see that as the risen Christ lifted Mary Magdalene from the depths of despair and the valley of hopelessness, so can He do likewise for us. May our faith in Him and His victories over the devil and sin, the grave and death, transform the darkness which hovers over us in this present life, into the blessed light of peace and assurance that all is well. AMEN.

(For the continuation of this Prayer, see "PRAYER" on page 2 in the Suggestions segment)

<u>Hymn</u>: "Christ the Lord Is Risen Today"

Do Not Be Faithless, but Believing

Hymn: "Crown Him with Many Crowns"

Scripture Lesson: John 20: 19-29

Sermon: "Do Not Be Faithless, but Believing"

"I cannot believe. Nor will I believe, unless I touch the crucifixion marks on His Body. Who could believe anything so unnatural as the resurrection of a man from the grave?"

Our Scripture Lesson speaks of "Doubting Thomas," one of the Twelve! Thomas was a plain, practical, matter-of-fact man, unable to grasp the supernatural; a man who could not accept the testimony of his friends, and a man who required direct personal evidence.

Thomas remained alone in miserable uncertainty for eight full days. The others told him Jesus had risen, but he simply could not believe it. The One he had loved so dearly was now gone from his sight forever. The Kingdom he had hoped for had also perished.

Then, Thomas joined the others. While assembled, the risen Lord appeared to them. Jesus said, "Peace be with you."

Jesus then focused His attention on Thomas. How well He knew the weak and strong points of His followers. He knew Thomas was deeply troubled. One observes the Lord's love in this incident because of His willingness to help Thomas overcome his doubt.

The test Thomas demanded was now before him. However, the Bible does not tell us Thomas applied the test. We are led to believe Thomas had sufficient proof simply seeing the nail and spear wounds, looking at the face, and hearing the voice he knew so well.

Thomas had been satisfied. He possessed the proof he needed. Thomas cried, *"My Lord and God!"*

This confession of faith came from the depths of Thomas's heart. This is revealed by the fact that Thomas became a missionary in India, where he built a church and suffered martyrdom by means of a spear.

We can be grateful there was such a man as Thomas among the disciples. He proved that they were not merely a group of gullible people, deluded by their hopes and dreams of a dead Master living again. Thomas could call the risen Christ "my Lord and God" because a fact too good to hope for, had became too certain to reject.

After Jesus enabled Thomas to overcome his doubt, He said to him, "Thomas, you believe because you have seen Me. Blessed are those who have not seen Me, and yet believe."

Do you believe Jesus Christ rose from the dead?

If you do believe, then why are you troubled? Why are you burdened with worry and fear, guilt and loneliness? Why are you burdened with any form of anxiety? Anxiety does not speak well of your faith.

Our faith shall be tested many times. It is tested when we, likened unto Thomas, doubt the promises of Jesus. And we will always be tempted to doubt His promises, because Satan is always planting and nourishing the seeds of doubt within us.

But as Jesus dealt with Thomas, so does He lovingly deal with us. So we might be faithful and believing that he sends us the Holy Spirit. If we make reading the Word of God and listening to this Word part of our daily life, the Holy Spirit will make it possible for us to believe, even though we have not seen. The Holy Spirit will enable us to feel light as light; Truth as Truth.

Through the years, thousands upon thousands have never seen, yet they believed. They took what faith they had, and they trusted the risen Christ to show them the way forward. They were truly blessed!

Let us do likewise. Through the Work of the Holy Spirit, let us see the power and love of a living Savior. Jesus Christ lives!

"He lives to bless me with His love,
To plea for me above,
My hungry soul to feed,
To help in time of need.

He lives to grant me rich supply,
To guide me with His eye,
To comfort me when faint,
To hear my soul's complaint.

He lives to silence all my fears,
To wipe away my tears,
To calm my troubled heart,
All blessings to impart.

He lives and grants me daily breath,
He lives and I shall conquer death,
He lives my mansion to prepare,
He lives to bring me safely there."

My friends, be not faithless, but believing! Blessed are you, if you have not seen and yet believe!

Prayer:

Lord God, each new day the prince of darkness plants the seed of doubt and uncertainty within our hearts. He is forever attempting to win us to his side. We believe, but we need Your assistance to help us overcome our unbelief. We therefore beseech you to let Your Spirit be ever with us. Direct us to Jesus Christ. Although we have not seen, make us believing, not faithless. By Your Grace, enable us to receive Him as our living Savior. As He made Doubting Thomas His humble confessor, grant that He may do likewise for us. Bless us with the light which only He can give, so we do not stumble along life's way. AMEN.

(For the continuation of this prayer, see "PRAYER" on page 2 in the Suggestions segment)

Hymn: "He Lives"

In a Little While

Hymn: "O God, Our Help in Ages Past"

Scripture Lesson: Psalm 34: 17-22

Sermon: "In a Little While"

Is it not true? We have all lamented the loss of a loved one; become anxious over a physical affliction or despondent because of daily pressures. The human heart can become burdened with any number of anxieties.

We all experience sorrow and distress. Whenever you and I encounter such anxieties, we can follow one of three courses. We can give way to despair and sour on the world. We can endeavor to drown our sorrow in substance, attempt to escape by living a life of waywardness. Or, we can turn to God.

Giving way to despair and turning sour on the world only makes the individual more miserable than he was before.

Attempting to drown your sorrows in drink or drugs will only produce an empty pocketbook and a big headache. Trying to escape your distress by living a life of waywardness will only create a guilty conscience.

Indeed, man's only hope in time of need is to turn to God!

The Lord Jesus said to His followers, "In a little while you will not see Me, and again, in a little while you will see Me, because I go to the Father. You will be deeply distressed, but your pain will be turned into joy."

To clarify His Words, Jesus gives a simple illustration. "When a woman gives birth to a child, she certainly knows pain when her time comes. Yet, as soon as she has given birth to the child, she no longer remembers her agony. The joy of giving birth to a child replaces any distress and pain she might have had."

Hence, Jesus reveals that we will have a season of sorrow and distress to pass through. But He also reveals that this sorrow and distress will eventually be turned into joy.

It is vital we remember that Jesus Christ has gone before us. He has prepared a place for all who love and believe Him. He assures all His followers that in a "little while," we will see Him face to face. And our hearts will thrill with an everlasting joy, which no one can take from us.

"A little while." Take these Words home with you! Meditate upon them, especially in time of need. These precious Words are given by a loving Savior to His faithful followers. If the prosperous can enjoy their riches only for a "little while," so shall the poor only carry their burdens for a "little while."

"In a little while you will see Me. I have gone to prepare a place for you." A few years here in a lowly dwelling, and then, a home in the Palace of the King of Kings. That affliction which no earthly physician can cure will soon be cured by the Divine Physician.

"In a little while you will see Me." The sight of Him shall, in an instant, wipe away all the memories of the darkest hours we experience in this life.

But as these Words give troubled hearts comfort, so do they serve as a trumpet call to duty. To what use are you putting the "little while" which has been entrusted to you? To live a life in which one is only concerned with self, is wasting this "little while." To live a life of idleness, enjoying whatever worldly treasure you possess, is a worthless life soon spent.

Exactly how are we to spend this "little while?" The Holy Spirit will tell us what we should do, by way of the Holy Scriptures. This is why daily Bible reading is so important.

Truly, your only hope in time of need is to turn to God. He will assure you through Jesus Christ that your distress and sorrow will be turned into joy; a joy no one can take from you.

My friends, "In a little while!"

Prayer:

Heavenly Father, we thank and praise You. You transformed the "little while" of the sadness and defeat of Your Son's crucifixion into the joy and victory of the Resurrection. We pray You fill us with Your Holy Spirit. Help us remember that Jesus Christ has gone before us. He has prepared a Place for all who love and believe in Him. Strengthen our faith in His promises, especially during dark hours of affliction and pain, sorrow and fear, perplexity and adversity. Through Him, give us the assurance that in a "little while" our trials and tribulation will be transformed into eternal joy. AMEN.

(For the continuation of this prayer, see "PRAYER" on page 2 in the Suggestions segment)

Hymn: "Close to Thee"

Come Up from the Basement

Hymn: "Standing on the Promises"

Scripture Lesson: Romans 5: 1-5, Philippians 4: 4-7

Sermon: "Come Up from the Basement"

A story is told about a father showing his daughter Hunt's famous painting, *"The Light of the World."* He explained to her that the door on which Jesus was knocking could only be opened from within. The latch was on the inside of the door. The little girl asked, "Daddy, why don't they let Jesus in?"

"I don't know," replied the father.

A few moments later, she said, "Daddy, I know why they don't let Jesus in. They live in the basement and can't hear him knock."

Out of the mouth of a babe, comes a great truth!

So many of us dwell beneath the darkness of this materialistic and anxiety-filled world. How much more peaceful our lives would be if we stopped living in the basement — if, with the help of the Holy Spirit, we raised ourselves Heavenward, through the Living Christ!

The Bible tells us that a small group of people from all walks of life was assembled in a room. Their Beloved Master and Friend had been crucified. Their hearts were heavy. They were filled with gloom. Their minds were overcome by the cares of this world. They knew the days before them would be filled with affliction and tribulation. They were choked with the fear of death. They were living in the basement of anxiety.

Suddenly, the Risen Christ was standing in the midst of them! Jesus said, "Peace, be with you." The troubled and tortured souls immediately became calm and peaceful.

Likened unto the followers of Jesus assembled many years ago, you and I are experiencing our share of anxiety. Some of us are overcome by the cares of this world. Some of us travel a difficult road. Some of us encounter thorns in the flesh. Some of us are choked by the fear of death. Likened unto the early followers of Jesus, we too possess heavy hearts! We are living in the basement.

But, let me assure you: Regardless of how much anxiety you encounter, you can come up from the basement, with the help of the Holy Spirit. If you throw open the door of your heart and allow the Resurrected Christ to enter, His peace will be with you — a peace which passeth all human understanding.

Jesus has risen from the dead! All is well! He offers you the fullness of His Grace and Love. He offers you complete and absolute reconciliation with the Father in Heaven. He offers you eternal life! Believe thou this? If you do, what more is needed to calm your troubled heart?

As St. Paul says: "Who shall separate us from the Love of Christ? Shall tribulation, or distress, or persecution, or famine, or nakedness, or peril, or sword? Nay, in all these things we are more than conquerors through Him that loved us. For I am persuaded, that neither death, nor life, nor angels, nor Principalities, nor power, not things present, nor things to come, nor height, nor depth, nor any other creature, shall be able to separate us from the Love of God, which is in Christ Jesus, our Lord."

My friends, I have conducted Worship Services at nursing homes for years. The residents have always requested the same hymn.

I ask you: has anyone traveled the bumpy road of life? Has anyone been tossed about by the troublesome waves of the world? Has anyone been pulled down into the depths of anxiety? Has anyone been in the basement more than these senior citizens? They have been well-seasoned. Yet, you should see — as I have seen — the glorious expressions on their faces as they sing:

"What a friend we have in Jesus,
All our sins and grief to bear.
What a privilege to carry,
Everything to God in prayer.
O what peace we often forfeit,

O what needless pain we bear.
All because we do not carry,
Everything to God in Prayer.

Have we trials and temptations?
Is there trouble anywhere?
We should never be discouraged,
Take it to the Lord in prayer.
Can we find a Friend so faithful?
Who will all our sorrows share?
Jesus knows our every weakness,
Take it to the Lord in prayer.

Are we weak and heavy laden,
Cumbered with a load of care?
Precious Savior, still our refuge,
Take it to the Lord in prayer.
Do thy friends despise, forsake thee?
Take it to the Lord in prayer,
In His arms He'll take and shield thee,
Thou wilt find a solace there."

Prayer:

Lord help us always come to You in prayer. The troublesome waves of life are constantly tossing us to and fro. We are overcome by worldly care and choked by endless fears. Our hearts become heavy with burdens. We begin living in the basement of anxiety. By Your Grace, give us Your Spirit. Direct us to Your Son, our Lord and Savior Jesus Christ. Grant that His Words and promises may give us Peace – that Peace which the world cannot give. AMEN.

(For the continuation of this prayer, see "PRAYER" on page 2 in the Suggestions segment)

Hymn: "Savior, Again to Thy Dear Name We Raise"

Prepared for the Storms

Hymn: "Jesus, Savior, Pilot Me."

Scripture Lesson: John 20: 26-31

Sermon: "Prepared for the Storms"

Have you ever considered how our lives are to be likened unto the weather? The sun shines. Then, suddenly: a frightening thunderstorm; a terrifying hurricane; a menacing snow blizzard. One moment, all is calm and peaceful; the next, trial and tribulation, affliction and anxiety.

Our journey through this life has been, and will continue to be, interrupted by storms of one description or another. We may be sunbathing upon the deck of a boat, when the ship hits a destructive obstacle. Resting in our seats, when the airplane crashes. Enjoying the beautiful scenery, when another automobile collides with ours.

We know not when the storm will strike — when lightning will tear our hearts with fear — when thunder will make our bodies tremble.

As long as the sun is shining and everything remains calm and peaceful, all is well. But when the storm strikes and the weight of helplessness is abruptly placed upon our shoulders, how do we react? When the clouds of darkness overshadow you, do you quickly throw your hands up in despair? Do you panic?

Not if the Angel's declaration that "Unto you a Savior has been born," has made any significant impact upon your heart and mind. If the coming of the Lord Jesus Christ is permitted to play a prominent role within your life, you will be prepared for the storms which come your way.

Be assured, Christ Jesus came into this world of ours so that through Him, we might overcome.

We are told in the 8th chapter of the Gospel of Saint Matthew, verses 23-27, that the Lord was weary from His endless labors. He therefore invited His disciples to join Him on a relaxing boat cruise. As soon as the boat was launched, Jesus became so relaxed that He went to sleep.

However, while He slept, a terrifying storm sprang into existence. The boat was tossed to and fro. The small vessel was literally swamped by waves.

Such storms were common on the Sea of Galilee. Its waters were many feet below sea level, and the surrounding mountains were so situated, their deep valleys acted like funnels for any rush of wind.

Needless to say, the disciples were filled with fear. They certainly thought the end was near. Helplessly they woke the Master, shouting, "Save us, Lord, or we shall perish."

Jesus replied, "Why are you so frightened, you men of little faith?" Then the Master rose to His feet. He rebuked the wind and the waters, and there was a great calm. At the same time, the disciples experienced an amazing stillness within their hearts. Overflowing with astonishment, they said several times, "What sort of man is this, that even the winds and the sea obey Him?"

After seriously considering what had transpired, the disciples must have experienced some form of embarrassment. Their Master had been with them. Yet, where was their faith? Why had they questioned His love and power?

The moral of this story is indeed a simple one. If Christ Jesus is with us, we are safe.

He will deliver us from any storm which may strike. His life and death revealed beyond any doubt that no storm was too great for Him. He cured the afflicted and healed the sick. He raised the dead and defeated the devil, and the evil forces which surrounded Him. He obtained victory over death for those who believe in Him.

My friends, as our clothing and homes protect us against the elements of nature's storms, so does our faith in Christ Jesus become our protection against the storms of life.

Therefore, do not possess a wick which only burns daily. Do not give your anxieties a chair to sit upon. For if you react to life's storms in this manner, you are only questioning our Lord's love and power.

Only believe — believe from the depth of your heart, mind, and soul that Jesus Christ has the power to overcome your trials and tribulations, regardless of their duration.

Be assured He will respond graciously to any urgent and earnest appeal from those He loves so dearly. When the time is right, He will say, "Be still," and the sun will shine once again.

Prayer:

Father in Heaven, grant us Your Grace, so we may never question the love and power of Your Son, Jesus Christ our Lord and Savior. Give us such a true, abiding faith in Him that we may always become the benefactors of His precious promises. Remove from us all doubts, so that the storms of this present life will not flood our minds with faithless fears and worldly anxieties. Give us Your Holy Spirit so we may have the assurance that whenever we approach Jesus with believing hearts, He will sustain our hunger and thirst, and overcome our trials and tribulations in accordance with Your Holy Will. AMEN.

(For the continuation of this Prayer, see "PRAYER" on page 2 in the Suggestions segment)

Hymn: "In the Hour of Trial"

Overcoming

Hymn: "O Holy Spirit, Enter In"

Scripture Lesson: Romans 8: 5-8, Galatians 5: 19-24

Sermon: "Overcoming"

It is said that the construction of a certain bridge was hampered by an old ship embedded in the bottom of the river. Powerful engines, steel cables, and derricks were unable to remove the obstacle. Finally, a young engineer suggested that the ends of a barge be fastened to the sunken wreck at low tide. When the tide rose, so did the barge, bringing the submerged relic with it. The obstacle was removed because the engineer had used the power of the ocean tide.

In the 3rd chapter of Ephesians, the Apostle Paul offers a prayer. He prays "that the Holy Spirit may work with power within you."

Paul conveys that no man can overcome obstacles he encounters by his own efforts. He must link his effort to overcome with the limitless power of God.

The lives we live, the world to which we belong, present us with countless concerns. We become frustrated by daily routine — worried about health, fearful about old age, troubled by human associations. We become engrossed in any number of self-concerns. We cater to endless anxieties. Self- centeredness becomes our major obstacle. Our devotion to self becomes the obstacle which hinders devotion to God. It becomes a barricade to physical and mental well-being. It becomes an obstruction to well-adjusted human relationships.

We need to remember; the Holy Spirit instills great power within us. It is indeed a thrilling moment at Boulder Dam when someone throws the switch, and the available power becomes actual power. This is what you and I must do. We must discover how to make the available, the actual. But how? How do we throw the switch in the spiritual realm? How do we release the potential power within us, so we might overcome? The answer: through our *faith* and *hope*.

Christian faith is acceptance of Jesus Christ as Lord and Savior. Faith is saying *"yes"* and *"amen"* to the message and the promises of Christ Jesus. It is the giving of ourselves to Him in trust and confidence. It is relying upon Him as a child relies upon his parents. An unshakeable faith in Jesus Christ is the Work of the Holy Spirit. If our faith does not give us the power we need to overcome, we must, with the help of the Hold Spirit, nourish it. Neglecting our Bibles, shunning meditation, failing to indulge in prayer, will not give us the nourishment we seek.

With *faith* comes *hope*. Hope involves the future. And the hope for the future which Christ Jesus promises those who believe and follow Him, ought to overcome numerous self-inflicted obstacles.

Who among us does not encounter obstacles? If we are not to become victims of unrestrained anxieties, we must rely upon our Christian faith and hope.

God, through Jesus Christ and the Work of the Holy Spirit, has given us a reservoir of water — shall we go thirsty?

He is prepared to give us untold energy — shall we operate on nerves?

He has shown us the Way — shall we take the narrow path covered with thorn bushes?

He has placed at our disposal a check — a check that will make us secure for life. Shall we cash it and live on its income? *Or*, shall we go on being insecure?

My friends, may the power of the Holy Spirit work within you. And may the work of the Holy Spirit continuously direct you to the Lord Jesus Christ.

<u>Prayer</u>: Heavenly Father, we humbly pray that You mercifully look upon the obstacles we encounter as we journey through this life. Send us Your Holy Spirit. Guide and direct. Nourish and sustain. Comfort and strengthen. Give us a true faith in Christ Jesus. Grant that His Way and Truth may dominate our lives. Enable the hope He gives to help us overcome. Grant us that we always feel Your Loving Presence. AMEN.

(For the continuation of this Prayer, see "PRAYER" on page 2 in the Suggestions segment)

Hymn: "Christians, Dost Thou See Them"

You are Precious to Him

Hymn: "How Great Thou Art"

Scripture Lesson: Luke 15:11-32

Sermon: "You are Precious to Him"

We often hear and read about a child being lost. We all share the anguish and heartache of his or her parents. But when the child is found, there is truly great joy.

In the 15th chapter of Saint Luke's Gospel, we are told that the publicans and sinners drew near Jesus to hear Him. The Scribes and Pharisees were shocked by this scene. They believed righteousness meant separating yourself from sinners. Thus, they were overwhelmed at seeing Jesus, Who professed to be righteous, mingling with the unrighteous. Is not a man's true character revealed by the company he keeps?

Unfortunately, many today share this same attitude. They refuse to mingle with certain individuals — with certain classes and races — because they feel superior.

In response to the murmurings of these religious leaders, Jesus tells the parables of "The Lost Sheep" and "The Lost Coin." He tells these stories to convey that such an attitude cannot prevail in God's children.

Jesus says to the Scribes and Pharisees, "Who among you, losing a sheep, would not seek it? What woman losing a coin would not search diligently through the house for it? Who among you, losing anything of value, would not look for it until it was found? Surely a lost man is more precious, and demands more urgent seeking, than a lost sheep or coin. And his recovery gives a fuller joy. I have been sent to seek and save *lost people.* How can I possibly fulfill this mission — how can I find that which is lost, unless I search for it until it is found? This is why I am with publicans and sinners."

It is well to keep in mind that we have all wandered astray. Even the most faithful among us have permitted loneliness and fear, selfishness and self-pity, worldly desire and anxiety, to carry us from the path of righteousness. Let him who has not walked the path of unrighteousness, cast the first stone.

The parables of the lost sheep and the lost coin paint a vivid picture of how much God cares. It is He that Hath made us. We are His — we are the sheep of His pasture. He has unsurpassed love for each member of His flock. He has created us to be His. But if we become lost, of what value are we to Him? The Shepherd cannot reveal his love to a lost sheep. The lost money is out of circulation. It has no value until it is recovered.

How God must suffer when we go our own wretched way — when one of His sheep hardens his heart and sinks out of the reach of His love.

But God's love for those who have wandered astray, leads Him to seek them until they are found — until they are restored. He seeks through His Son Jesus Christ, Who came not to be ministered unto, but to minister. He seeks through the Voice of the Holy Spirit within man's heart. He seeks through His Church — His Word and Sacraments. He seeks through His children.

God commands His children to GO and SEEK! Are you seeking? Through you, God wants to bring the Way and the Truth to others. Through you, He wants to give comfort to those in need. Through your examples of love and actions of mercy, He seeks His lost sheep.

Will God find those He so diligently seeks?

Those who want to be found; will be found. But woe be unto those who neither care nor feel the need for belonging to God's Family. Woe be unto those who will not heed the Voice of the Holy Spirit with their hearts. Woe be unto those who will not permit the light of Jesus Christ to penetrate the darkness in which they live.

For those who are found, the heavens will echo with shouts of rejoicing. The joy of the Heavenly Father over one sinner returning to the flock will indeed be great!

My friends, if you have wandered astray — remember, God cares. He cares about what will happen to you. He cares about what will happen to all His lost sheep. Do you care?

Prayer:

Heavenly Father, we thank You for the gift of Your Son Jesus Christ, whom You have sent to seek and save the lost. Grant us Your Holy Spirit, so we may see Him as our Shepherd — as the door by which we enter your Heavenly Home. Through Him, You have revealed how precious we are to You. As He has loved us, help us to care for the many needy souls who surround us. Give us faith and zeal, so we may more earnestly desire and more diligently seek our salvation through Him as well as the salvation of our fellow man. Make us vessels of His Grace, examples of His teachings, and witnesses of His Truth and Glory. AMEN.

(For the continuation of this Prayer, see "PRAYER" on page 2 in the Suggestions segment)

Hymn: "Softly and Tenderly"

Does It Really Matter What You Believe?

Hymn: "Come, Holy Ghost, Our Souls Inspire"

Scripture Lesson: Hebrews 11: 1-39

Sermon: "Does It Really Matter What You Believe?"

Does it really matter what you believe?

What you believe, navigates your life. What you believe controls the thoughts you think, the words you speak, and the deeds you perform. What you believe has affected your past, is affecting your present, and will affect your future.

What you and I believe, determines how we live. Your life is a revelation of what you believe.

For example, Columbus believed the world was round. Adolf Hitler believed he could conquer the world. Martin Luther believed the Church needed to undergo a reformation. These men lived accordingly.

The 9th chapter of the Gospel of Saint Luke, verses 18-20, tells us that Jesus asked His disciples, "Who do the people say I am?" The disciples replied, "Some say you are John the Baptist. Others say you are Elijah. Still others say you are one of the old prophets who have come to life again." Then Jesus asked His disciples, "Who do you say I am?" And Peter said: "Thou art the Christ."

When Jesus first met Peter, he was a fisherman. He was a rough, unpolished personality. He was quick to make blunders, quick to speak his mind, and quick to act. But in spite of these characteristics, Jesus promised to make Peter a "fisher of men."

At the time Peter made his confession, "Thou art the Christ," his faith in Jesus had not fully blossomed. There can be little doubt; there was much he did not understand.

However, Peter nourished his faith by listening attentively to his Master's Words. As the life of Jesus unfolded, Peter's love and trust — his understanding of the Nazarene — matured.

Peter believed this man from Nazareth had come from, and was of, God. He believed Jesus was the Promised Messiah, Lord and Master, Savior and Redeemer. He believed Jesus was the Way and the Truth — the revealer of God's new covenant with man.

Yes, Peter believed that Jesus was the Christ, and lived accordingly.

After Jesus ascended into Heaven, Peter played a vital role in the development of the Christian Church. The big, unsophisticated fisherman became a great preacher. The Holy Spirit used one of his sermons as the means to convert three thousand souls. No other sermon has been known to be responsible for the conversion of so many individuals at one time.

Although there is much doubt among scholars as to whether Peter actually wrote a New Testament Book, there appears to be much agreement that he was a major contributor to several of the News Testament authors. We can, therefore, say with assurance that even in this 21st century, the effects of Peter's ministry can still be strongly felt.

Wherever he went, Peter carried the Gospel of his Lord with him. He opened the door to the Gentiles. He comforted the sick. He gave hope to the dying. He helped provide for the needy. He cared for the afflicted. His convictions enabled him to stand firm against the physical and mental adversaries he encountered. No fear nor worry, no sickness nor affliction, no pain nor sorrow could detach him from his Master's cause. He was imprisoned twice, and assaulted on several occasions, as the result of his faith in Jesus.

Tradition tells us that Peter was condemned to death by crucifixion. He requested to be crucified head downward. He felt unworthy to die upon a cross in the same manner as did his Lord.

Truly, Peter was a dedicated and devoted follower and disciple. He was indeed a strong pillar of the Church. He did what he did simply because he believed in the Lord Jesus Christ. His convictions made him a vigorous, consistent, and courageous Christian.

My friends, let us be likened unto the Apostle Peter. Let us focus our attention upon the Words of the Lord, believe in His promises, and be directed by His Gospel.

It does matter what you believe. Your life is a revelation of what you believe. What you believe, will determine how you live.

If you truly and sincerely believe in the Lord Jesus Christ, you will live accordingly. And if you live accordingly, be assured, the Savior of men will not fail you.

Prayer:

Heavenly Father, we believe, but help us overcome our unbelief. Fill our hearts and minds with Your Holy Spirit, so that likened unto Peter and the other Apostles, we will always accept Your Son, Jesus Christ, as Lord and Master — Savior and Redeemer — Revealer of Your New Covenant with men. Help our lives to be navigated by His Gospel — by His Words and promises — when we encounter the raging storms of fear and worry, sickness and afflictions, pain and sorrow. Permit our faith in Him to enable us to stand firm against the physical and mental adversaries we all encounter. And wherever we go, help us to carry the Gospel of Christ Jesus with us. Help us by way of our Christian examples and words, to give hope to those in need of hope, to comfort those in need of comfort, and to care for those in need of care. AMEN.

(For the continuation of this Prayer, see "PRAYER" on page 2 in the Suggestions segment)

Hymn: "O Take My Hand, Dear Father"

Stop and Investigate

Hymn: "Thou Art the Way"

Scripture Lesson: Luke 12:34-40

Sermon: "Stop and Investigate"

The red and white stop sign is familiar to all. It is found at almost every intersection. The sign commands the driver to stop his vehicle, and to investigate before proceeding. But how many of us always heed this sign as conscientiously as we should? Perhaps we have been fortunate so far. However, is it not true that our carelessness can lead to disaster?

So with the Word of God we are told to STOP and INVESTIGATE, but we go merrily on our way.

In the 10th chapter of I Corinthians, the Apostle Paul gives us a warning. He says, "Let anyone who thinks he stands take heed, lest he fall."

Paul cautions us that what happened to the Israelites of long ago could very easily happen to us. He directs our attention to the Exodus.

Paul reminds us how God liberated Israel from the brickyards in Egypt — how He sustained them during their trials in the wilderness. But in spite of all God did for His children, many failed to please Him, and left their bones in the desert.

The Israelites set their course toward the Promised Land. They all became partakers of God's Divine Grace and Favor. Unfortunately, many had no corresponding realization of the responsibility that accompanies such a privilege. Many refused to take their relationship with God seriously. They expressed ingratitude. They gave way to idolatry; to moral decay. They doubted God's power to provide for them. They provoked God. They put Him to the test. They gave way to discontentment and grumbling. Needless to say, God was not pleased. Therefore, many Israelites perished in the wilderness.

Paul is frank and fearless as he speaks. Unless we exert caution, history will repeat itself.

God's new act of deliverance is through the Lord Jesus Christ. When you and I were baptized, we set our course toward the "Promised Land." Are we still following this course? Should we not STOP and INVESTIGATE?

Let what happened to the Israelites stand as an example for us. Let us be cautious about self-complacency and false security. The overconfident individual loses Divine Grace.

God demands much more from us than merely confessing we are Christians. Although we have been baptized and have received Holy Communion, we can still be destroyed. Did not the Israelites sit down to eat and drink spiritual food, and then rise up to play? What does the Bible say? Many of them left their bones in the desert.

The Lord promises no immunity to the person who follows Him. No Christian is ever safe from trial and testing. Even the strongest among us is in danger.

Likened unto the Israelites, we are also tempted to take God's love and grace for granted — tempted to cling to whatever satisfies the desires of the flesh — tempted to test and doubt the Creator's power — tempted to give way to discontentment and grumbling.

Our reaction to the temptations we encounter is the heart and core of Paul's concern. We are told, "You may have done well so far, but look out — you will encounter more temptations. Take heed, lest you fall. It happened before; it can happen again."

Guard you heart and mind. The mischief will begin in these two areas. The journey is hard, but you need not fall. We are not left to battle by ourselves. Through the Lord Jesus and the Work of the Holy Spirit, we can overcome.

The Lord says, "Believe Me. Trust Me. Be faithful. Come to Me, you who are heavy laden, and I will give you rest."

Paul tells us: No temptation confronts you that is not common to man. There is no temptation without a way of escape. There is no burden without the strength to bear it. There is no hardship that with God's help, we cannot endure.

We have an unfailing resource. If we stand alone, the enemy will surely overpower us. Therefore, lean on God. His grace, His weapons, will see us through.

My friends, we have all seen adventure stories in which someone appeared to have no way of escape. In complete suspense, we wondered, *will he make it*?

Will you make it? Will you enter the "Promised Land?"

Before you answer this question, STOP and INVESTIGATE! Let anyone who thinks he stands; take heed, lest he fall!

Prayer:

Heavenly Father, Who is the strength of the weak and the comfort of the needy, we beseech You to be with us as we journey upon life's road. Guide and direct us by Your Holy Spirit, so we might "stop" and "investigate" before proceeding. Grant we take heed, lest we fall. Grant we do not regard our sins lightly or lose ourselves in overconfidence. Grant that we daily bring forth the fruits of repentance and amend our lives. Make us strong to resist the ways of the world. Enable Your Son, Jesus Christ our Lord and Savior, to show us the Way of escape when we are tempted, and give us the strength to endure the burdens we bear. Through Him, help us always to please You, that when this life has run its course, we may enter the Promised Land and be Yours forever more. AMEN.

(For the continuation of this Prayer, see "PRAYER" on page 2 in the Suggestions segment)

Hymn: "Jesus, the Very Thought of Thee"

The Loving Father

Hymn: "For the Beauty of the Earth"

Scripture Lesson: Psalm 100

Sermon: "The Loving Father"

Let us focus attention upon One Who is by far the most loving of all fathers, yet One Who appears to be the least appreciated. He is certainly the most deserving of His children's gratitude, affection, and devotion, yet countless members of His family give extremely little, if any, thought to Him. Truly, our thoughtlessness — our piecemeal, lukewarm and halfhearted response to the Heavenly Father's Blessings, which never cease to flow unto us in endless abundance — must prove to be exceedingly painful to Him.

Our text is an expression of thanksgiving used by the Israelites of long ago, especially by the woman of the household as she drew the water required for her family's daily needs from the community well.

Although drawing water from the well was an everyday chore, the common things of life became occasions of religious celebration for many of the Old Testament Israelites. The well's life-giving water was a symbol of God's saving powers. Therefore, as the women would draw water from the well, they would sing, as recorded in the 12th chapter of Isaiah, Verses 3-6:

"With joy I shall draw water from the well of salvation. Because of His bounteous goodness — because of this saving power which the Lord God places at my disposal, I shall give thanks to Him. I shall call upon His Name. I shall make known His deeds among the nations. I shall proclaim that His Name is exalted. I shall sing praises to Him for the glorious things He has done. I shall reveal my joy and gratitude in all the earth. I shall shout and sing for joy. For the Lord God is in our midst."

Hence, voice was given by the Israelites to the gratitude in their human hearts for the Heavenly Father's manifold Blessings.

But what has happened to this voice in our 21st century? Is this voice of thanksgiving disappearing? If so, why? Certainly, we have so very much more to be thankful for than the Israelites of whom we speak.

We are part of a dry and thirsty land. And you and I have contributed our share to making this land what it is. We live in a land of sin — a land of fear and hatred, sorrow and heartache, loneliness and frustration, trouble and despair. We live in a land of great human need. How desperately we yearn for the source which will enable us to surmount.

We do not want running streams or brooks, which are full in the spring and dry in the summer. We want wells that will sustain us year-round.

The Heavenly Father freely gives us these wells. And these wells are easily accessible to all. No matter how unworthy the individual may be, he may draw whatever amount of water he needs.

The water necessary to quench our needs flows to us through the Work of Jesus Christ. The Savior of men says, "If anyone thirst and believes in Me, let Him come to Me and drink. Whoever drinks the water I give him will overcome his thirst. The water I give him will become in him a spring of water welling up to eternal life."

The water of salvation flows to us through Christ Jesus. And by the influence of the Holy Spirit, you and I are made willing to partake of this water.

Drinking deeply of what Jesus Christ gives makes us new creatures. As the man lost in the hot desert begins to revive the moment the precious water touches his lips, so does the Gospel of Jesus Christ impart new life to the soul as soon as it caresses the heart and mind of the needy. If given the opportunity, this Gospel can implant such power into the human being that he becomes enabled to overcome all worldly barriers.

Truly, the Father in Heaven has abundantly placed His wells of life-giving blessing at our feet. He graciously invites you and me to draw whatever amount of this water we deem necessary. Shall we be foolish? Shall we refuse to accept His generous invitation and despise His love and grace, mercy and compassion?

OR shall we, with joy, lavishly draw water from His wells? And if we do partake, shall we not thank Him with hearts and hands and voices?

My friends, the Father in Heaven has created us. He daily sustains our physical, mental, and spiritual needs. He is our deliverer and salvation, refuge and strength. He is always willing to guide us whenever we become perplexed, and always ready to free us from all our ills. Who can number the manifold gifts of love He has so generously showered upon His children? As the result of His gift to us in Christ Jesus, He has given us a hope which can never be surpassed. Does not the awareness of knowing there is Someone who cares so much for each and every one of us, move us — like the Israelites of long ago — to give voice to the gratitude which should be embedded within our hearts and minds?

Prayer

Dear Father in Heaven, our creator and sustainer, we Your children and sheep of Your pasture give You our unfeigned thanks. We thank You for the endless fruits which You have so generously provided for the nourishment of our bodies, minds, and souls. We thank You for the roof over our heads, kindred to love, and friends to cherish. We thank You for the green world in which to live and the air to breathe. Indeed, there is no limit or boundary to the blessings for which we can be thankful for. But above all, we thank You for the Work of Your Holy Spirit and the faith He brings into existence. We thank You for the victory of peace and joy which can be obtained through Christ Jesus. Guide and direct us to Your life-saving wells which You have so abundantly placed at our disposal. And always help us to drink deeply, so our needs may be satisfied. AMEN.

(For the continuation of this Prayer, see "PRAYER" on page 2 in the Suggestions segment)

Hymn: "Now Thank We All Our God"

The Secret of Peace

Hymn: "Jesus Lover of My Soul"

Scripture Lesson: Psalm 23

Sermon: "The Secret of Peace"

Jesus says:

> "I am the bread of life. He that cometh to Me shall never hunger. He that believeth in Me shall never thirst."
>
> "Come to Me. I will give you rest. I will not leave you comfortless."
>
> "I am the Good Shepherd. I have come to minister unto you."
>
> "I am the Door — the Way — the Truth — the Life."
>
> "Let not your heart be troubled — all power has been given to Me."

Jesus tells us these things and many more. Why? In the 16th chapter of Saint John's Gospel, Jesus says, "I have told you these things that through Me, you will have peace of heart. Here on earth, you will have many trials and tribulations. But be of good cheer. Remember, I have overcome the world."

In this world, we do experience trial and tribulation. We all experience affliction, sickness, pain, worry, loneliness — the list is endless. We all experience darkness in one form or another. All human beings must bear the load — some in greater degrees than others.

No one knows the trial and tribulation one must endure in this world better than Jesus. He experienced all we experience and a great deal more. But He always committed Himself into the hands of the loving Father in Heaven. And He always overcame.

God never promised us all sunshine. He never promised an earthly life free of burdens. He doesn't leave us by ourselves. He doesn't leave us without help. He sent us his son Jesus, that through Him we might overcome. The key to our overcoming is our faith in Jesus Christ! The doorway to peace in this life is believing Jesus is our Savior; is total trust in His promises.

The promises of Jesus give the believer a peace which this world cannot give. His promises give the believer refreshment — give light in the midst of darkness. The promises of Jesus make the believer realize; the suffering of this present time cannot be compared to the Glory that awaits him. Our faith in Jesus, our faith in His promises, will give us divine strength to endure.

Truly, God does not promise all sunshine. But then — all sunshine makes a desert. Your trials and tribulations are the testing grounds of your faith. Let us be likened unto the Apostle Paul. His thorn in the flesh brought him closer to Jesus. His faith was strengthened through His weakness. Our thorns enable us to be living demonstrations of Christ's power within us.

Jesus loves you. He revealed how much He loves you from His Cross on Calvary. On Easter morning, He overcame the world. Through Him, you can also overcome. Therefore, do not allow the things of this world, whatever they may be — the fears of today, nor the worries about tomorrow — to separate you from the love of Jesus. Through Him, overwhelming victory can be yours.

My friends, whatever your load — come to Jesus. Come with a believing heart.

Jesus says, "I will give you peace. Remember, I have overcome the world."

<u>Prayer</u>:

Father in Heaven, You know the valleys of darkness through which we must travel along this earthly road of trial and tribulation. We know You care for us. You are our refuge and strength. We pray You, therefore, to preserve us from the temptations of our enemy. Help us in every time of physical or mental or spiritual danger, to lift our hearts and souls unto You. Grant us Your Grace. Send us Your Holy Spirit. Give us a deep, sustaining faith in Your Son Jesus Christ, who has overcome the world — so through Him, we can also overcome. Minister unto us through His example and promises. Let nothing in this world separate us from Him, nor from Peace and Glory, which await those who are faithful to Him. AMEN.

(For the continuation of this Prayer, see "PRAYER" on page 2 in the Suggestions segment)

Hymn: "Standing on the Promises"

Crossing the River

Hymn: "Nearer, My God to Thee"

Scripture Lesson: John 14: 1-6

Sermon: "Crossing the River"

Someone said, "I want to reach the Promised Land without going through the wilderness."

How true this is for so many of us. We also want to reach the "Promised Land," but we do not want to pay attention to the Lord's teachings as we cross the river of life.

The fact remains; it is impossible to cross this river — to enter the promised land — without the Heavenly Father's guidance.

Unless we depend solely upon the Heavenly Father's assistance, we shall never see the wondrous paradise He has prepared for His children.

In the 3rd chapter of the Old Testament Book of Joshua, we are told that the Israelites had made camp on one of the banks of the Jordan. All they had to do to enter the land of milk and honey, where a richer life awaited them, was to cross the river. This certainly does not sound like it would be a complicated and difficult task.

But unfortunately, it was April and the Jordan was swollen by the spring rains and the melted snow from the nearby mountaintops. The overflowing river with its swift current made the Jordan impossible to cross by normal means.

What did the Israelites do? How did they ever manage to enter the Promised Land? Joshua had taken the problem to the Lord. And God supplied His children with the answer to their need.

The Lord God said to Joshua, "Take up the Ark of the Covenant, and pass on before the people that they might know that as I was with Moses, so shall I be with you now." The Ark contained the two stone tablets upon which the Law of God had been recorded. It symbolized the Lord's presence.

Joshua said to his people, "Come and hear the Words of the Lord your God. Today you shall know that the Living God is among you. He will guide and protect you. See the Ark of the Covenant. It shall pass before you into Jordan. You shall follow it. When soles of the priest's feet that carry the Ark touch the water, the river shall be stopped from flowing. The waters coming down from above shall stand in one place."

The people did as they were commanded. They followed the Ark so that they would know the way. The very moment the priest's feet touched the Jordan, the approaching water ceased to flow. The water flowing away from the people disappeared. And the Israelites walked upon dry ground into the Promised Land. Truly, this was a venture which could not have been accomplished without the omnipotent powers of the Almighty God.

Now, in this 21st century, we find ourselves in the same situation as the Israelites of long ago. Here we stand on one side of the river. On the other side is the "Promised Land." And be assured, to attempt to cross this river on our own without the guidance and direction of the Heavenly Father — without the assistance of His omnipotent powers, without His mercy and grace — will only prove disastrous. We shall surely be destroyed.

Although the swift current of the river can quickly destroy, the loving Heavenly Father is ready to help those who want to enter the "Promised Land" to cross without harm or injury. He has given us the Lord Jesus Christ, Who is the Way. He has given us the Holy Spirit so we might better understand the Way. And He has also given us the Holy Scriptures and the Church — and the power of prayer, to nourish and prepare us for the countless emergencies we shall encounter on the way.

Indeed, God is not dead. He is living among us. He is help in time of trial. We can lean on Him in time of weakness or fear. His ear is open to the cry of the needy. He "who never slumbers or sleeps" has promised, "Lo, I shall be with you always, even unto the end of the world."

My friends, the Lord is your light and salvation. Will you not believe? Will you not trust and obey Him? He can be your strength and hope. Let Him take you by your hand. He will overcome the barriers in your path. He will lead you across the river into the "Promised Land," where a richer life awaits.

Prayer:

O Lord God, we thank You. You have given us Your only begotten Son, Jesus Christ. Through Him we are enabled to safely cross the river of this present life, and finally enter into the land You have promised to all your faithful children. We ask You to always give us Your Holy Spirit. Guide and direct us by Your mercy and grace that we may feed upon the bread Christ Jesus so freely gives. By so doing we shall surely, according to the promises, dwell in the eternal Heavenly Mansion which awaits all who love and worship You. There we will experience freedom from the pains and affliction, trials and tribulations, which presently engulf our lives. AMEN.

(For the continuation of this Prayer, see "PRAYER" on page 2 in the Suggestions segment)

Hymn: "He Leadeth Me"

The Power of the Human Tongue

Hymn: "Yield Not to Temptation"

Scripture Lesson: James 3: 2-12

Sermon: "The Power of the Human Tongue"

Let us take a close look at the world in which we live. What do we see?

We see conflict between nations; dissension between neighbors. We see animosity between husband and wife; friction between parents and children; strife between brother and sister. We see malice in the mind; pain and sorrow in the heart.

Indeed, man's relationship with one another is a serious problem.

Now I ask you, what do you believe is one of the major contributors to this problem? I believe it is the human tongue.

As we are all aware, the tongue is located on the floor of the mouth. It enables man to speak, which is the means man uses to express himself.

In the 3rd chapter of the Epistle of James, we are told, "The man who professes he never says the wrong thing, can consider himself perfect. For if he can control his tongue, he can control every part of his personality."

Strange, is it not? We can control all kinds of beasts and birds, reptiles and sea creatures. We can control atomic energy. We can control NASA flights to the moon and beyond. How difficult we find it to control our tongues.

And a tongue out of control is a destructive instrument. It is likened unto a spark of fire, which sets acres and acres of forests ablaze. It creates so much damage that man is unable to repair its destruction.

A tongue, out of control, is likened unto the sting of a small insect or the bite of a snake. It inflames the blood, irritates the whole system, and converts day and night into restless misery. The unclean, slanderous, critical words the tongue can speak are more harmful than deadly poison and slice deeper than any knife.

I suppose you and I will never know the sorrow and bitterness, pain and heartache, our tongues have created. There is no doubt: The human tongue can be the devil's best ally.

Yet, on the other hand, the tongue can be one of God's richest blessings. It can calm. It can heal. It can build. If controlled, it can prove very beneficial.

Whether you tongue is bitter or sweet, a curse or a blessing — whether it promotes evil or good — depends on you.

Truly, your tongue has great power!

It can inflame a mob to riot or inspire a group to compassion.

It can start quarrels, inflict heartaches, destroy friendships and break up homes. OR it can rescue souls from despair, strike powerful blows for justice, and start feet marching toward the goal of brotherhood.

Your tongue can be the best part of you, or the worst. You must exert great caution when you employ this tool of speech. One cannot stress enough how vital it is to keep the tongue under control at all times.

It is true; keeping control of your tongue is a difficult task. But it is also true, our faith in Jesus Christ — our Christian convictions — ought to give us the control we need. If not, our God-man relationship isn't what it should be. Tongue trouble comes from heart trouble. The secret of overcoming it is not in sealed lips, but in sanctified hearts.

The Lord God says;

> "By your words, you shall be condemned or justified."
>
> "A word fitly spoken is like apples of gold in pictures of silver."
>
> Speak every word for someone's edification, that it may minister grace."

My friends, remember: How Christian we are in our relationships, depends upon how well we control that small tool of speech located on the floor of the mouth.

Prayer:

Lord God, we beseech You, forgive us for the unclean, slanderous, and critical words we have allowed our tongues to speak. Forgive us for the pain and heartache, sorrow and bitterness we have inflicted. Fill us with Your Holy Spirit. Guide and direct us to Jesus. Fill our hearts with His love and willingness to forgive — His patience and understanding. In our relationships with others, help us follow His example. Help us use our tongues to promote good, and to minister Your Grace. AMEN.

(For the continuation of this Prayer, see "PRAYER" on page 2 in the Suggestions segment)

Hymn: "Living for Jesus"

Treasure Hunting

Hymn: "My Mother's Bible"

Scripture Lesson: Luke 11: 27-28, Isaiah 34: 16a, Psalm 43:3

Sermon: "Treasure Hunting"

Throughout history, man has relentlessly attempted to obtain treasure. Kings gambled the lives of their subjects to secure wealth from foreign powers. Men sailed to new lands seeking precious metals, in spite of the hardships involved. Countless prospectors surrendered all, even life, attempting to locate gold and silver.

Today, man continues his search for worldly treasures. This is revealed by his compulsion to speculate in various investments; by the record crowds at department stores on "Sales Day"; by the high rate of crime; by the irresistible longing to be successful in business and on top of the social ladder.

How much richer we would be if we searched for Heavenly treasures with the same eagerness, desire, determination, sweat, toil, and willingness to suffer that drives us to search for worldly treasures.

These Heavenly treasures are within the reach of everyone! They are given to us by God the Father, God the Son, and God the Holy Spirit. The Lord God is the giver. He patiently waits to give us His Holy Word, so we might know every good path — so we might experience peace and blessedness of the soul. The Lord God is the giver. We are the receivers.

In the 2nd chapter of the Book of Proverbs, we are told:

> "My son, if you receive My Words and treasure up My Commandments with you, making your ear attentive to wisdom and inclining your heart to understanding; if you cry out for insight and raise your voice for understanding; if you seek it like silver and search for it as for hidden treasure; Then you will understand the fear of the Lord and find the knowledge of God. Then you will understand righteousness and justice and equity — every good path. For the Lord Gives wisdom."

How do we come into possession of the Heavenly treasure of which we speak? The conditions of attainment are classified under three major steps.

The first step is to LISTEN. We must listen to what the Teacher has to say. We must listen to His Message.

How can we listen, if we continually classify our Holy Bibles as secondary reading material? We have time to glance at the local newspaper, to look at the latest issue of *Better Homes and Gardens* or *Newsweek*, to read secular novels. Yet, day after day, we completely ignore the Holy Scriptures.

The first step in the attainment of Heavenly treasure is to listen. The second step is to RETAIN what we have heard. When summer arrives, we do not throw our snow shovels away. We put them in storage, knowing the day will come when they will be useful. The same is true concerning the Word of God. The hearing of this Word will not bless us, if we do not store its truth within our hearts and minds.

How do we retain what we have heard? This brings us to the third step in the attainment of Heavenly treasures: REFLECTION. Reflection prevents forgetfulness. If we listen to a sermon on faith, and do not reflect this faith when a problem arises within our lives, then we are bound to forget whatever we have heard about faith in the first place.

We all seek treasure. Let us waste little time seeking the greatest of all treasures. You must seek in order to receive.

Those who find a few diamonds upon the surface do not bring their labor to a conclusion. They dig down beneath. They toil on for months and years. They do not cease if more can be gained. Hearing the Word of God is a mine, which yields on the surface. But we must not stop there. We must dig deep. We must continue to listen, retain, and reflect. LISTEN! RETAIN! REFLECT!

My friends, diligently search for the treasures only God can give. Search with the same eagerness; the same determination; the same desire; the same sweat; the same toil and willingness to suffer, with which you search for worldly treasures.

Jesus says, "Lay not up for yourselves treasure upon earth, where moth and rust consume — where thieves break in and steal. Rather, lay up for yourselves treasure in Heaven. For where your treasure is — there will your heart be also."

Prayer:

Lord, forgive us for not searching for what You so willingly give with the same eagerness and determination we employ in searching for what the world offers. Faith in You cometh by hearing Your Word. We have ears; help us hear. Help us to be likened unto newborn babes and desire the milk of what You have to say to us. Help us to seek with our whole heart the Treasure of treasures — to diligently study Your Holy Scriptures. Grant us Your Holy Spirit that our seeking may not be in vain. Grant that our seeking will enable Your Word to draw comfort and strength, especially in times of trial and temptation. Grant that Your Word will lift us in hope, make us strong in service to You and our fellow men, and fill us with true knowledge of your Son who is our Lord and Savior. Grant that we not only hear Your Word and retain Your word, but also reflect Your Word in our everyday lives. AMEN.

(For the continuation of this Prayer, see "PRAYER" on page 2 in the Suggestions segment)

Hymn: "Break Thou the Bread of Life"

A Diet That Nourishes

Hymn: "Wonderful Words of Life"

Scripture Lesson: Proverbs 2: 1-10

Sermon: "A Diet That Nourishes"

What certain foods do for our physical bodies, certain knowledge does for our well-being. Some categories of knowledge contribute a great deal to our welfare. Others contribute very little; a few, nothing at all; while some can prove very harmful.

In the 1st chapter of his Letter to the Colossians, the Apostle Paul tells his Christian brethren he will constantly pray for them. His Prayer will be threefold.

First, he prays they be filled with the knowledge of God's Will.

Second, he prays they use this knowledge to bring credit to their Lord's Name — to bring joy to His heart by bearing good fruit.

And third, he prays they be so strengthened by this knowledge, that they pass through any experience and endure it with courage.

Today, Saint Paul prays for you. He prays for me.

First, he prays that you and I be filled with knowledge of God's Will

Man has a great thirst for knowledge. He is eager to become acquainted with himself — with the wonders around him. Today, more than ever before, men are striving to satisfy this thirst. Scientists are racing against time to conquer the mysteries of space. Doctors are working around the clock to discover the secrets of disease. Learned men of all professions are constantly laboring to improve our ways of life. More people are receiving college degrees than ever before. There can be little doubt; 21st century man is making an all-out effort to increase his knowledge.

Unfortunately, in our struggle to obtain knowledge, the Will of Him Who has created us is neglected. Our world bears witness to this fact. We fail to realize that man may have knowledge of many things — but if he is ignorant of God's Will, he is ignorant of the purpose for which he was created. Knowledge of God's Will is the beginning of all true wisdom.

We may possess some knowledge concerning God's Will. Paul prays we increase this knowledge. In the 9th chapter of Saint Luke's Gospel, God Himself tells us, "This is My beloved Son Jesus Christ, My chosen one. Listen to Him!" How can we say we are listening to Jesus, if we consider Confirmation our graduation from religious instruction? How can we say we are seeking knowledge of God's Will if we do not daily meditate upon the Gospel of Him, Whom God has sent to us — if we only engage in private devotions when the mood moves us?

Second, Paul prays we use our knowledge of God's Will to bring credit to our Lord's Name — to bring joy to His heart by bearing good fruit.

Knowledge is of little use if gathered in a vain manner. It is of value only as one receives and uses it wisely. After all, of what benefit is it to hear the Word of God, and not heed it? If the knowledge of God's Will is to serve us, it must be applied to everyday life. How wisely one applies this knowledge is revealed by the fruit he produces.

And third, Paul prays we be so strengthened by the knowledge of God's Will, that we pass through any experience and endure it with courage.

We are well aware of the extra strength we need to endure the trials and heartaches life brings our way. Only Jesus Christ can give us the strength to march onward. Though we may be sensitive to pain and hardship, we shall, by the knowledge which the Holy Spirit instills in us, rejoice in the assurance of God's presence — rejoice in the absolute victory of His cause.

My friends, what certain foods do for our physical bodies, certain knowledge does for our well-being. Anyone who eliminates knowledge of God's Will from his diet is in serious trouble.

Remember, the foods we eat are worthless unless converted into fuel and energy — unless they build tissues and strengthen. So, too, with knowledge of God's Will. Unless we apply this knowledge to our daily lives, it is also worthless.

The better the food is, the stronger the body. The more intake of high food value, the better the body is equipped to resist physical afflictions and hardships. So, too, with knowledge of God's Will. The greater our intake, the better equipped we are to pass through any experience and endure it with courage — the easier it is to resist the many evil temptations we encounter.

The Apostle Paul prays for you! He prays you be filled with knowledge of God's Will. He prays you use this knowledge to bring credit to your Lord's Name — to bring joy to His heart by bearing good fruit. He prays you be so strengthened by this knowledge that you pass through any experience and endure it with courage.

Prayer:

Heavenly Father, help us answer Saint Paul's Prayer. Help us not live by bread alone, but by every Word that proceeded from Your Mouth. Make us wise. Although the grass withers and the flowers fade, Your Word will stand forever. Help us study and believe this Word. Fill us with Your Holy Spirit so this Word may be a lamp unto our feet and a light unto our path. Grant that through Your Son Jesus Christ, our Lord and Savior, we seek knowledge of You as we would search for silver and gold. Grant we hold fast and use this knowledge, knowing it is life. Grant we be so strengthened by our knowledge of You, our peace and joy shall be full. AMEN.

(For the continuation of this Prayer, see "PRAYER" on page 2 in the Suggestions segment)

Hymn: "Guide Me, O Thou Great Jehovah"

Faulty Foundations

Hymn: "Rock of Ages"

Scripture Lesson: Matthew 17: 1-5

Sermon: "Faulty Foundations"

After the Saint Francis Dam in California collapsed in 1928, just 2 years after its completion, a Special Commission was established to investigate the cause. Following this investigation, it was concluded that the tragedy had resulted from a faulty foundation. This defective construction brought various forms of disaster to thousands of people. Four hundred and fifty lost their lives. Others suffered physical and material damage.

Unfortunately, such horrible incidents happen.

A *faulty foundation* is the explanation for the downfall of so many people when put to any kind of test. It is the explanation for the physical and moral, mental and spiritual collapse of countless individuals. It is the explanation as to why millions encounter calamity and misfortune in their lives. It is the explanation as to why juvenile delinquency and vandalism, crime and suicide, drug addiction and alcoholism, materialism and self-centeredness, hopelessness and human anxiety are on the rise.

Faulty foundations— a grave threat to human existence!

As Jesus completed His famous Sermon on the Mount, He said, as recorded in the 7th chapter of the Gospel of Saint Matthew, "Everyone who hears these Words of Mine and puts them into practice, is like a wise man who built his house upon the rock.... And everyone who hears these Words of Mine and does not put them into practice is to be likened unto a foolish man who built his house upon the sand."

Jesus speaks about two different men. One is wise. He plans his house with his eye upon the future. The other is foolish. He gives no thought to the future. He only thinks in terms of the present.

The wise man permits the Lord Jesus Christ to be his architect. He allows the Savior of men to be his blueprint. He hears the Words of the Lord and applies them to his everyday life. He listens, believes and obeys. He builds upon a foundation of rock that will withstand any test.

On the other hand, the foolish man permits the things of this world to become his architect. Worldly possessions, pleasures, and comforts become his blueprint. He has no time for Christ Jesus. He hears the Words of the Lord, but he does not obey them. He does not put them into daily practice. He does not trust the Lord's promises to nourish and sustain him. He does not allow the Holy Spirit to develop a conquering faith within his heart. He builds upon a faulty foundation, and as soon as his house is put to the test, disaster and calamity strike. His house is simply unable to withstand the storms that rage against it.

Have you ever watched a small child amuse himself on a beach? He erects a miniature house upon the sand. But what happens to this house when the high tide puts it to a test? It is completely destroyed.

In this life we now live, you and I shall indeed encounter many temptations and endless trials and tribulations. The sun does not always shine. The sky is not always blue. We are tested time and time again. But whether we withstand these tests depends upon our foundation. If we have built upon the rock, we have nothing to fear.

However, if we devote our hearts to building upon a faulty foundation, our temptations become uncontrollable; our trials and afflictions become tearing anxieties; our tribulations and sufferings become nightmares. Life falls apart!

Be assured, only the house that has been built upon the rock will survive that supreme test, the day we stand before Jesus Christ to give an account of our lives. The house built upon a faulty foundation will surely collapse. And great will be its fall!

My friends, every minute of every day, you and I are in the process of building. Are you dedicating your energies to building upon the rock, or upon the sand?

Whether you stand or fall when the dark clouds of life come your way — whether you stand or fall on the Great Judgment Day — depends entirely upon your relationship with the Lord Jesus Christ, here and now!

Blessed is the man who hears the Words of Jesus and puts them into practice.

Blessed is the man who is not a hearer only, but a doer as well.

Jesus said, "Everyone who hears these Words of Mine and puts them into practice, is like a wise man who built his house upon the rock.... And everyone who hears these Words of Mine and does not put them into practice is to be likened unto a foolish man who built his house upon the sand. The rain fell. The floods came. The winds blew and beat against that house — and it fell. And great was the fall of it."

Prayer:

Lord God, we beseech You to help us overcome our foolish ways. Fill our hearts with Your Holy Spirit. Continually direct us to Your Son, Jesus. Make Him our rock. Make Him our architect and blueprint. Make Him the potter. Make us His clay. Make His Words the foundation upon which we build. Through Him, support our weaknesses and sustain our needs. Through Him, enable all things to work together for our everlasting salvation. AMEN.

(For the continuation of this Prayer, see "PRAYER" on page 2 in the Suggestions segment)

Hymn: "How Firm a Foundation"

A Book to be Read

Hymn: "Break Thou the Bread of Life"

Scripture Lesson: Matthew 4:4

Sermon: "A Book to be Read"

During the 14th century, John Wycliffe translated the Latin Vulgate into English, so that all men might have the opportunity to read the Bible. There were those who were willing to make great sacrifices to obtain a few chapters of one of Saint Paul's Epistles.

What price would you be willing to pay for a few chapters of this Book?

Do you recall, in days gone by, the esteem in which our grandmothers and grandfathers held their Bibles? Do you recall how they would sit in their favorite chairs and read the Bible to themselves, or to one another? This was how many Christians spent a portion of their evenings.

But most don't spend their evenings this way anymore. Times have changed. Tractors have replaced the workhorse. Automobiles have replaced the buggy. Computers have replaced office workers and technicians. Could it be possible that an abundance of social activities, secular reading materials, cell phones, television, and computers have replaced the Bible?

It is true; there is still a great demand for the Bible. This is revealed by the fact that it continues to be a best seller. However, it appears too many are purchasing this Book not to read, but to exhibit as a showpiece or a status symbol.

How many of you can honestly say the Bible is your companion? When was the last time you picked up the Holy Bible for the purpose of reading it?

A woman remarked, "I let my minister read the Bible for me on Sunday mornings. After all, he understands it much better than I do." Is this as close as we come to the Bible?

What are we attempting to say? We are simply saying that the Holy Bible can be of little value to the man or woman who possesses it, but makes no effort to read it.

The Lord Jesus says, "If you continue in My Word, you shall know the Truth." But how can you and I possibly know the Truth, if we continue to neglect this Word? And if we are not guided by the Truth revealed unto us by the Son of God, we shall be guided by our own human emotions.

Is it any wonder why our world is so full of anxiety and moral decay — why self-centeredness and materialism are setting today's pace? Far too many personalities are being guided by their human emotions, rather than by the Holy Scriptures.

What is the Bible? It is the Word of God. It is a means by which the Creator speaks to men about His relationship with us, and about our relationship with our fellow man.

Truly, the Bible is "The Book of Life." It is a map which directs us along the road of this present life. It is the food which sustains us as we make life's journey. It is the armor and the weapon that transcend all life's battles.

The Bible contains the answers to our hopelessness and helplessness — to our fears and problems. It is a window through which we can see God the Father, God the Son and God the Holy Spirit, working within the arena of human history. Through the Holy Scriptures, we see an eternal life which surpasses all human anticipation.

Through the centuries, the Bible has played a vital role in the lives of men. This Book has converted entire communities. It has released countless individuals from fear and superstition. It has fostered education and care of the needy. It has stimulated loving family life and honest government. It has transformed many a wilderness into a beautiful garden.

Whenever and wherever the Bible has been withheld, darkness and oppression have taken over.

Let us again ask the question: "When was the last time you picked up your Bible for the purpose of reading it?"

You say you read your Bible 'occasionally' or 'when you have the time.' Suppose you fed a newborn infant only occasionally, or whenever you had time. Would the child grow and develop as he should? Chances are, under such treatment, the infant would die.

Can you honestly expect your life in Jesus to survive, to grow and develop, under the indifferent treatment you are presently giving it?

Simply complaining about your problems and decrying moral conditions, passing more laws and making changes in political administrations, cannot solve many of today's problems. However, daily Bible reading and the application of God's Word to our everyday lives will.

My friends, make reading your Bible a daily practice. As you study and meditate upon this Book, you may encounter an awakening. Is this not what you want? Is this not what our present world needs?

Jesus says, "If you continue in My Word, you shall know the Truth. And this Truth will make you free."

Prayer:

Lord God, our Creator and Sustainer, we humbly thank You for Your gift of the Bible. We beseech You to help us always revere, love, and treasure Your Holy Scriptures. Help us overcome the hardness and carelessness of our hearts, and implant within us the desire to read and study them. With the help of Your Spirit, grant that Your Precious Word will enable us to find Jesus and fill us with eternal hope. Grant that the Holy Scriptures will comfort and sustain us along life's way, and flood our dark lives with Heavenly Light. AMEN.

(For the continuation of this Prayer, see "PRAYER" on page 2 in the Suggestions segment)

Hymn: "Wonderful Words of Life"

A Mutual Characteristic

Hymn: "Alleluia! Sing to Jesus"

Scripture Lesson: Psalm 46

Sermon: "A Mutual Characteristic"

Have you ever considered how we have come from different homes and therefore possess different backgrounds? We have different physical features and personalities; different attitudes and habits; different talents and interests. Who can number the differences which exist between human beings?

Yet, in spite of all our differences, we share one common problem. We all encounter various forms of anxiety.

Fortunately, we have the answer to this mutual problem. The author of I Peter gives us the solution. He prescribes that we be humble, be trustful, and be watchful.

First, we are told to "clothe ourselves with humility and to serve one another. The Lord God is always against the proud, but always ready to bestow His Blessings upon the humble. So humble yourselves under God's Mighty Hand, and in His own good time, He will lift you up."

The question is: How does being humble overcome our cares and concerns?

Humility opposes self-confidence. The independence of the self-reliant individual leads him to believe that he can sustain himself. Therefore, he has little room in his life for God and his fellow man.

On the other hand, the humble person recognizes that by himself, he is merely a simple creature. He realizes the role God plays within his life. It is because of his God-man relationship that he sees his need for his brethren, and their need for him.

Humility does not degrade an individual, as is commonly implied.

Humility is an esteemed virtue; in that it helps the individual to better comprehend his purpose in life. This understanding leads the humble person to apply his God-given Gifts, not only to self, but to others as well.

If we, therefore, humble ourselves and minister unto those in need as the Almighty God directs us, we will have little time to think about self. The blessings we shall receive by following God's commands will enable us to rise above our trials and tribulations.

Secondly, the author of I Peter encourages us to "cast all our burdens upon the Lord, knowing that He cares for us."

How do we know that God cares? Did He not create us? Did He not send us His Son Jesus Christ, so we might have light to overcome our darkness?

Through Christ Jesus, the Father in Heaven has assured us "that not even a sparrow falls to the ground without His attention ... that the very hairs upon our heads are numbered ... that there is joy in His Presence over one sinner that repents."

Can there be any doubt concerning God's Love for you? What, therefore, is preventing you from casting your burdens upon Him? Do not hold onto your apprehensions any longer than you would hold onto a red-hot iron!

Thirdly, the writer of I Peter implores us to "be watchful and self-controlled, for our enemy the devil is always about, prowling around like a hungry lion roaring for its prey. *Resist him. Stand firm in your faith.*"

In this world, we are living in the midst of a war between good and evil. Evil temptations are constantly bombarding us. With great zeal, the devil is ever attempting to gain entrance into our lives. We must be on a constant alert. For if we in any way drop our guard, we are giving Satan the opportunity to flood our lives with darkness.

My friends, we share the same common problem. We all encounter various forms of anxiety.

Luther has said: "Although you cannot stop the birds from flying over your heads, you can stop them from building a nest in your hair."

Although you and I shall continue to encounter misgivings and apprehensions, if we pay heed to the author of I Peter, we can prevent these same misgivings and apprehensions from building a nest within our hearts and minds.

We are told to be humble, to be trustful, to be watchful.

“And after we have endured our cares and anxieties for a little while, the Lord God, Who has called us to share His Eternal Glory through Christ Jesus, will make us strong and secure. All power is His for ever and ever."

Prayer:

O Lord God, You know the dark places our lives must pass. We ask that when we enter them, we be filled with Your Holy Spirit, so we may always look to You, our refuge and strength. Whenever any danger threatens the health and peace of our physical, mental, and spiritual beings, grant that the hope of Your Mercy may never fail us, and the consciousness of Your love may never be clouded or hidden from our eyes. Help us to be humble when we have the tendency to think only of self; to be trustful when some burden assails us; to be watchful and strong, so we resist Satan and his effort to flood our hearts and minds with darkness. AMEN.

(For the continuation of this Prayer, see “PRAYER” on page 2 in the Suggestions segment)

Hymn: “Praise to the Lord, the Almighty”

God Will Take Care of You

Hymn: "I Need Thee Every Hour"

Scripture Lesson: Romans 8: 31-39

Sermon: "God Will Take Care of You"

A story familiar to all — a story which should bring much comfort to each one of us — is the Old Testament narration of the Israelite's wilderness journey.

God's children had crossed the Red Sea. The Lord had delivered His people from their bondage to the Egyptian Pharaohs. The great Exodus had begun.

However, before the Israelites could reach the Promised Land of Milk and Honey, they had to journey through the wilderness. The problems they had encountered in Egypt had been conquered. But the harshness and risk of life they would endure in the wilderness was still before them. The march would be long; the climate would be unbearable; the fatigue would be great. The needs, burdens and sacrifices, hardships and anxieties they would experience before reaching the Promised Land, still remained inescapable facts. This journey would indeed be one of faith.

The great Exodus continued.

After traveling three days in the wilderness, the Israelites developed an overpowering thirst. They discovered springs, but the water was unfit to drink. Moses, on behalf of the people, cried unto the Lord, and God made the bitter water sweet.

Many days later, a similar incident occurred. Again Moses cried unto the Lord, and God made water flow from a rock, satisfying everyone's thirst.

Approximately 45 days after the Israelites began their wilderness journey, they developed a great hunger. Again Moses cried unto the Lord, and God provided quail and small wafers made from desert trees and shrubs.

During the wilderness journey, the needs of God's children were many. But the Lord was with them. He always found a way to provide in abundance. And because of His love and grace, the Israelites reached the Promised Land.

The journey of the Israelites through the wilderness is to be compared to our journey through life. Our destination is the Promised Land. However, as we walk this road, we shall discover ruts and stones in the path. The march will appear to be long; the climate shall become unbearable; the fatigue will be great. We shall hunger and thirst. The load will be heavy at times. The needs and burdens, sacrifices and hardships, will be many.

But whatever you do, do not become discouraged. Like Moses in the wilderness, cast your cares upon the Lord with a believing heart. He cares for you. The Lord walks with you. His love and grace will sustain, protect, and guide you along life's way.

My friends, before we can reach the "Promised Land," we must pass through the wilderness. As you make this earthy journey, remember: God will take care of you.

Prayer:

Dear Lord, our needs are many. You know the deep places our lives experience. Help us when we enter them to be likened unto the Israelites. Help us cast our cares upon You, knowing You care for us. Only You can find a way to provide for us in abundance. Only Your love and grace will enable us to reach the Promised Land — the Land of Milk and Honey, the Heavenly Mansion that Jesus has prepared for all who love and trust You. As we pass through the wilderness, as we make this earthly journey, give us Your Holy Spirit so we have the faith and assurance You will take care of us along life's way. Help us always to fight the good fight. AMEN.

(For the continuation of this Prayer, see "PRAYER" on page 2 in the Suggestions segment)

Hymn: "I Heard the Voice of Jesus Say"

Are You Hiding Your Light?

Hymn: "Lord, Speak to Me, That I May Speak"

Scripture Lesson: Matthew 5: 14-16

Sermon: "Are You Hiding Your Light?"

How vividly I remember when, as a boy, my entire Sunday school would assemble in the nave of the church so we might together conclude our morning session by saying, "Let your light so shine before all men, that they may see your good works, and glorify your Father in heaven."

Through the years, this Bible verse has served as a real guiding star.

As followers of Jesus, we become the light of the world. It was for this reason that Jesus came into our world. He came to shed light to overcome the darkness. As His followers, we are to reflect this light. In His Sermon on the Mount, Jesus makes it quite clear that our calling is to be light-bearers — that our light is to shine freely and without hindrance before all men.

I fear, however, that many of us are hiding our light under a bucket. When in contact with those surrounding us, we attempt to keep our faith a big secret, for fear of being ridiculed or embarrassed.

We fail to realize that our lives are open books, telling a story. Every word we speak, every act we perform, tell others what we think of the Christ we profess to follow. Our lives are leading others either closer to or farther away from the Kingdom of God.

What kind of story are you telling with your life?

Is it not true, we sing, "God Himself is Present," but fail to speak and act accordingly? We sing, "Sweet Hour of Prayer," and content ourselves with a short prayer – if any at all. We sing, "O for a Thousand Tongues," and are not willing to use the one we have. We sing, "Blest be the Tie That Binds," and permit the least offence to destroy this tie. We sing, "Serve the Lord with Gladness," and then gripe about what we have to do. We sing, "Thou Art the Way," and continue to go the way of the world.

We sing, "Cast Thy Burden upon the Lord," and worry ourselves into nervous breakdowns. We sing, "My Faith Looks Up to Thee," and continue to trust in ourselves. We sing, "O Jesus, Thou Art Standing, Outside the Fast Closed Doors," and continue to keep the doors to our hearts closed, because they are already filled and overflowing with self-pity and countless anxieties. We sing, "I Love to Tell the Story," but never mention this story to those who have need of hearing it. May the Heavenly Father forgive us.

Indeed, we have a great responsibility. We are the light of the world. Our light must be seen by all men; so they might glorify the Father above Who is the author and giver of this light. To fulfill our calling, we must think of ourselves as being lamps of God.

A lamp without light is useless. To obtain the light we need, we must surrender our hearts and minds and souls to Jesus Christ. Our lives must reflect His presence.

In order to keep our lights burning, they must have a source of fuel. Gathering this fuel will not be difficult. Is it so difficult to open our Bibles, to pray and meditate?

As God's lamps, we must radiate abundant and glorious light. To function properly, a lamp must be trimmed daily. Each new day, we must cut away those worldly desires and affections which will hinder and prevent our lights from burning brightly.

Then, we must place ourselves where our light will do the most good. We live in a dark world — a world full of great need. We live in a world full of ignorance, error and unbelief, vice and crime. To overcome this darkness, we must reflect the light of Christ Jesus by way of our testimonies, exhortations, and examples.

My friends, if you profess to be a disciple of the Lord Jesus Christ, an instrument of the Holy Spirit, a Lamp of God; do not hide your light under a bucket. Do not keep your faith a secret.

You are the light of the world. You are the only hope this world has. Therefore, let your life radiate a spirit of love and good will — a spirit of helpfulness and mercy — a spirit of understanding and forgiveness.

Let no one say to you: "It is because you have shown me in your life such a dismal and unhappy picture of Christianity that it has never looked the least bit attractive or appealing to me."

"Let your light so shine before all men, that they may see your good works, and glorify your Father in Heaven."

Let your light so shine among others, that they may also discover the loving and merciful Heavenly Father as revealed to us in the Person of Jesus Christ.

Prayer:

Almighty God, inspire us by Your Spirit to conform our wills unto Your Will. Make us Your lamps and permit our lights to shine brightly before all men. Take our lives and lips, and speak through them to Your Kingdom's spread. Take our possessions and use them to Your blessed purpose. So possess our hearts and minds that wherever we are, whatever we do; we may comfort and minister unto the suffering, friendless, and needy.

May we be instruments of You through which others may come to know and glorify You. Make us vessels of Your Son's grace, examples of His teachings, and witnesses of His truth and glory. May all we do reflect His presence. AMEN.

(For the continuation of this Prayer, see "PRAYER" on page 2 in the Suggestions segment)

Hymn: "Stand up, Stand Up for Jesus"

The Fruit of a True Christian

Hymn: "O Jesus, I Have Promised"

Scripture Lesson: John 13: 34-35

Sermon: "The Fruit of a True Christian"

Let us direct our attention to the 13th chapter of 1 Corinthians, verses 1-8. The Apostle Paul says:

> "If I speak in the tongues of men and of angels, but have not love, I am a noisy gong or clanging cymbal. And if I have prophetic powers, and understand all mysteries and all knowledge, and if I have all faith, so as to remove mountains, but have not love, I am nothing. If I give away all I have, and if I deliver my body to be burned, but have not love, I gain nothing."

In essence, Paul is stating that the individual who professes to be a Christian, and who goes through all the outward motions of a Christian, is only deceiving himself if he does not have love in his heart and love for the living creatures which surround him. If we do not possess this love of which Saint Paul speaks, what we do or say will become likened unto crashing cymbals. We will clang and clang. We will create a great deal of noise, but this noise will simply be loud, empty, and meaningless.

How many of us, on various occasions, camouflage our real motives when helping to bring comfort to a needy neighbor? And then, we waste little time in hitting the gong and crashing the cymbals. We make plenty of noise, so others might become aware of what we have done.

However, if the motive behind our deed was not love, then we can be assured that we have gained absolutely nothing, regardless of how much noise we make. And if our true motive was love, we would not create noise in the first place.

Love is the foundation of any Christian. It is the basic ingredient of Christianity. Love enables man to fulfill the purpose for which he was created. It is the keystone of all character. Love is to be compared to the keystone in the center of the arch. This stone holds the others in place and keeps the arch strong and beautiful. Remove this stone, and the arch falls.

But, let us proceed with caution when employing the term of love. There can be little doubt that there exists different kinds of love. There is human and divine love. There is imperfect and perfect love. Actually, these different kinds of love can be classified within three categories.

First, there is Eros, or human love. I will love, but only as long as I receive something in return for my love. Needless to say, this love never attains perfection.

Second, there is Filial love. This is a love which exists between parents and children. Although Filial comes close to being perfect, it cannot attain perfection inasmuch as it contains elements of Eros. I love, but become extremely hurt or disappointed if I receive nothing in return for my love.

Third, there is Agape or divine Love. This is the only perfect love which exists. I love, expecting absolutely nothing in return for my love. But then it is not my love, but Christ Jesus loving through me. To attain this divine and perfect love, the Lord Jesus must dwell within us. He must be in complete command of the control center which governs the heart and soul. Agape love is the love of Christ translating itself into human expression. When confronted with decisions concerning others, the question always becomes not "what shall I do?", but rather, "What would Christ Jesus do through me?"

And it is this Agape love to which Saint Paul refers. "The love of Christ is the highest and best gift that man can possess. Since nothing is expected in return, this love is slow to lose patience. It looks for a way of being constructive. It is not possessive. It is not anxious to impress, nor does it cherish inflated ideas of its own importance. It has good manners and does not pursue selfish advantage. It is not touchy. It does not compile statistics of evil or gloat over the wickedness of other people. On the contrary, it is glad with all good men, when Truth prevails. This Perfect Love knows no limit to its endurance, no end to its trust, and no fading of its hope. It can and will outlast anything. It is in fact the one thing that still stands when all else has fallen."

My friends, it is essential to stress the fact that as Christians, our rule of life must be love — the love of Christ.

If you profess to be a Christian, if you go through all the outward motions expected of a Christian; you will only be deceiving yourself if you do not have the love of Christ in your heart and your life for the living creatures of God which surround you, whether the creature is white or black, yellow or red.

If you do not possess the love of Christ, what you do or say will be likened unto crashing cymbals. You will clang and clang. You will create noise in abundance; this noise will be loud, empty, and meaningless.

Prayer:

O God of love, Who has given us a new commandment that we should love You and one another as You love us, and gave Your only begotten Son for our life and salvation. Grant we may allow Jesus to so control our hearts and minds. His love will translate itself into human expression through us. Help us during times of special need, not to become overly demanding or self-centered martyrs. Help us not to be crashing cymbals, making loud and meaningless noise. Enable us to love those who touch our daily lives, especially the suffering and friendless, with the love of Christ which passes all human understanding. May His love saturate every fiber of our being. Give us His good manners and patience, kindness and understanding. Give us His willingness to forgive and forget, and His sincere thoughts and unselfishness. AMEN.

(For the continuation of this Prayer, see "PRAYER" on page 2 in the Suggestions segment)

Hymn: "Love Divine, All Loves Excelling"

The Shepherd and His Flock

Hymn: "Savior, Life a Shepherd Lead Us"

Scripture Lesson: Ezekiel 34: 11-16

Sermon: "The Shepherd and His Flock"

And Jesus said, "I am the Good Shepherd." What does this statement mean to you? Are you fully aware of its implications?

Shepherds and their flocks were indeed familiar scenes to Jesus. Unfortunately, our association with shepherds has become practically non-existent. Therefore, it might prove beneficial to review the relationship which exists between a shepherd and his flock.

A shepherd is one dedicated and devoted to the sheep entrusted to his care. Inasmuch as his sheep are in constant danger from thieves and animals, it is necessary for the shepherd to carry a stout club or rod. He also carries a long stick in his hand called a staff.

Not only does the shepherd have to protect his sheep from their enemies, he must also pay close attention to the general health and welfare of the flock. When his sheep have exhausted the pasture and the water supply in one area, he must lead them to better ground. He makes every effort to find those sheep which have wandered astray. He is watchful for stones which might hurt their feet; for pits into which they might fall. He binds their wounds and attempts to strengthen the weak and sick.

He encounters sleepless nights and physical exhaustion, the unrelenting elements of the weather, as well as long hours of hunger and thirst. He endures all this, and a great deal more, in order to provide for the countless needs of his sheep. If necessary, he is even prepared to surrender his life.

Certainly, it is not difficult to understand the close relationship which develops between a shepherd and his sheep. He comes to know their individual personalities and weaknesses; ailments and anxieties.

On the other hand, the sheep become extremely close to their shepherd. They become acquainted with his voice and appearance, ways and manners. They learn to trust, obey, and love him. They will not respond to a stranger. It is said that sheep enjoy their highest degree of well-being when they know their master is near.

Now let us return to our original question. Are you fully aware concerning the implication of the statement Jesus made, "I am the Good Shepherd"?

Jesus is simply stating that the relationship between the shepherd and his sheep is to be likened unto His relationship with His followers. In the 10th chapter of the Gospel of Saint John, verses 11-16, the Lord Jesus claims to be the perfect or ideal Shepherd.

First, Jesus claims to be the Good Shepherd on the grounds that He is not to be compared to a hireling. A hireling is an individual who has been employed to care for the sheep, and one who has no real interest in what he is doing. He simply waits for the time to pass so he can collect his wages. A hireling uses the sheep as nothing more than a means to reach a selfish end. Since he has not love for the sheep, he is not willing to take any risks for them. Therefore, when the wolf appears, the hireling is quick to disappear.

The wolf to which Jesus refers is the evil that exists within this world. This wolf may appear in various forms — as a seed of worry and despair, doubt and disbelief, greed and hatred. He may appear as popular heresy — as a tendency to ease morality — or in the form of any number of other human problems which may prove fatal to the sheep.

Jesus bases His claim of being the Good Shepherd not only upon His teaching or example or miracles, but also upon His Savior-hood. He gave His Life for the flock. He lovingly and willingly entered into a victorious battle against the destructive fangs of the wolf, so that you and I might have an eternal relationship with our Creator. He sacrificed everything and held back nothing in order to fulfill our endless needs. In other words, He did not leave us to our own fate, as a hireling would have done.

Second, Jesus professes to be the Good Shepherd on the grounds that He knows His sheep. He knows their individual personalities and weaknesses, ailments and anxieties. He knows His own and will sustain them.

And those who truly belong to His flock know Him. They know He is near and will sustain them, regardless of their need. They trust, obey, and love Him. And as a result of their faith in Him, they experience peace and a wondrous feeling of security.

Third, Jesus claims to be the Good Shepherd on the grounds that His heart goes out to other sheep who feel their need of Him. Not only are the Jews to whom He is speaking in our text the children of God, but so are the Gentiles. His saving gospel is also for them. All men, regardless of their color or race, social status or age, shall form One church — One flock under One Shepherd.

My friends, if it is your earnest desire, the Lord Jesus Christ will be your Shepherd. If He becomes your Shepherd:

You will not possess any wants.

He will make you lie down in green pastures.

He will lead you to peaceful and still waters.

He will restore your life and soul.

He will lead you to the path of righteousness.

And even though you may walk through the valley of death, you will not feel any evil.

For He will be with you.

He will protect and comfort you with His rod and staff.

He will prepare a table for you in the presence of your enemies.

He will anoint your head with oil.

Your cup will overflow.

Surely, goodness and mercy will always be with you.

For you will dwell in His Glorious Mansion forever.

Prayer:

O gracious and loving Heavenly Father, we are truly the sheep of Your pasture. How grateful we are for the Shepherd You have sent us in the Person of Christ Jesus. So that His coming may not be in vain, we as Your needy lambs beseech You to enable us through the work of Your Holy Spirit, to daily partake of the manifold blessings He is so willing to bestow upon us. May He help and sustain, guide and direct us during the trials and heartaches, pains and anxieties of this present life. Overshadow our hearts and souls, minds and bodies with His presence so we may always, through our faith in Him, draw the strength necessary to overcome our weaknesses and the healing powers needed to rise above our afflictions. AMEN.

(For the continuation of this Prayer, see "PRAYER" on page 2 in the Suggestions segment)

Hymn: "The Lord My Shepherd Is"

Put Your Trust in Jesus

Hymn: "A Mighty Fortress Is Our God"

Scripture Lesson: Psalm 118: 5-9

Sermon: "Put Your Trust in Jesus"

We humans are a strange lot. We daily entrust ourselves to countless man-made objects, knowing that man is an imperfect creature subject to never-ending mistakes. We place our confidence in bridges and skyscrapers; in airplanes and automobiles; in all manner of man-made objects.

Yet, day after day we suffer untold fears and anxieties, simply because we place so little trust in the promises of Jesus Christ.

In the 6th chapter of Saint John's Gospel, we are told Jesus and His disciples were on a mountainside. Five thousand people surrounded them. Many of these men, women, and children had traveled a great distance to see and hear Jesus. They were hungry. Their supply of food was gone. Surely some would collapse, if sent away without nourishment.

Jesus put Philip to the test. He asked His disciple, "Where can we buy enough food for these people to eat?" Without giving the matter serious thought, Philip replied, "Ten dollars' worth of bread would not be enough to feed this multitude." Unfortunately, likened unto so many of us, Philip thought only in terms of money as being the solution to the problem. But the fact remained: even if the group had enough money to purchase the necessary bread, where could they do so? They were in the wilderness.

If Philip had given the problem serious consideration, he would have replied, "Lord, only you can supply the multitude's need. You are the Bread of Life."

Philip had seen Jesus supply the needs of others. He had seen Jesus heal the sick and lame; restore the sight of the blind; raise the fallen. He had seen Jesus provide for the physical, mental, and spiritual needs of many. Philip knew that Jesus had the Power to perform miracles. But then, as we have stated, the disciple had not given the matter much thought.

We are told a boy in the crowd had a lunch basket containing five biscuits and two fish. Jesus commanded the multitude to sit down. The people obeyed without hesitation. Jesus took the five biscuits and two fish. After a short prayer of thanksgiving, He divided the food. He asked His disciples to distribute the portions He gave them. When the multitude had eaten, they were satisfied. And there were twelve baskets of food left over.

This miracle, as well as all the other miracles Jesus performed, should give us great comfort. Like the needy human beings surrounding Jesus on that mountainside, we also have needs. Our concerns may be about what we shall eat, what we shall drink, what we shall wear. It may be a burden resulting from affliction; guilt resulting from sin; anxiety resulting from trouble at work; heartache resulting from conflict with loved ones. This life is full of dark clouds.

What do we do when a storm comes our way? Many of us can be likened unto the disciple Philip. First, we do not think the matter through in the manner a Christian should. Second, we place too much emphasis upon money — upon what the world offers, as the means by which we can overcome. How foolish we are!

It is true that the world offers much. But it does not — it cannot — supply our every need. Only God can give us complete peace of heart and soul. He can give us what the world cannot give.

As the revealer of Truth said, "Little children, do not be anxious about your needs. Do not be anxious concerning what you shall eat, what you shall drink, what you shall wear. If God provides for the birds of the air and the plants of the field — will He not much more provide for you, O men of little faith? Therefore, do not be anxious, for your Heavenly Father knows what your needs are. Seek first His Kingdom and His Righteousness, and all your needs will be supplied."

The words "men of little faith" perhaps best summarize our greatest need. We pray, "Give us this day our daily bread." But what are we really praying? So many times, we pray nothing more than words.

Truly, we can learn much from that multitude surrounding Jesus on the mountainside. They had a need. Jesus commanded them to sit down. They obeyed without hesitation! They were nourished!

Let us also pay heed to the teachings and commands of Jesus Christ. He will work miracles in our lives, if we give Him the opportunity to do so. He gives His Word. He gives His grace to those who desire it. He is the nourishment needed to cope with the problems of this life. He feeds. He sustains. His store is never empty.

My friends, if you daily entrust yourself to all manner of man-made objects, knowing man is an imperfect creature subject to never-ending mistakes, then why do you not place more confidence and trust in the commands and promises of Jesus Christ?

Prayer:

Lord God, the storms of this life are many. Our needs are great. We encounter untold misery because we are quick to trust in ourselves and the things of this world, but slow to trust the One You have sent to nourish and revive us. Forgive our foolishness. Send us Your Holy Spirit. Grant we may see the errors of our ways. When we walk in the midst of trouble and the clouds of darkness hover over us, direct us to Your Son Jesus Christ. Make our faith in Him and His promises, our stronghold and fortress. Help us allow Him to minister unto our every need. He alone is our Shepherd — our refuge and strength. AMEN.

(For the continuation of this Prayer, see "PRAYER" on page 2 in the Suggestions segment)

Hymn: "What a Friend We Have in Jesus"

You Need Not Be Blind

Hymn: "Thou, Whose Almighty Word"

Scripture Lesson: Isaiah 40: 6-8

Sermon: "You Need Not Be Blind"

We have all encountered someone who did not possess the gift of physical sight. Do you recall your reaction to this experience?

You probably reacted with pity and sympathy — with compassion. For unlike us, a person without physical sight cannot behold the danger of this human life; the faces of his loved ones; the wonders of God's world.

I have often wondered if the blind are not better off in many ways than we who possess our physical sight. Perhaps it is they who should have compassion for us.

You and I can learn a great deal from the blind. Many blind individuals, such as Helen Keller, possess the eyes of faith. This faith allows them to see the wonders of the world, far more beautiful than the one we behold. We may possess our physical sight, but we are blind spiritually. We place our confidence in ourselves, in our human achievements, and in our worldly possessions. *We* are blind to the fact that only Jesus Christ can give us the sight which enables us to see those things that really count in this life.

In the 18th chapter of Saint Luke's Gospel, we are told that on the road to Jericho, there was a blind man. Day after day this man sat for hours, pleading, "Help me, help me, for I am blind." Day after day, he hoped those passing by would respond with a coin or two.

One day this man heard an unusual number of voices coming toward him. He inquired as to what was happening. He was told Jesus of Nazareth was approaching. The blind man had heard about Jesus and His miracles. Under normal circumstances, he could have reaped a good harvest from the passing caravan. But he knew his great opportunity had come.

Although he was unable to see, he could walk, he could cry aloud. Therefore, in spite of his handicap, he made his way toward Jesus. He gave little thought to the fact that he might be injured by the oncoming crowd. He raised his voice in prayer, "Jesus, Son of David — have mercy on me."

Those surrounding Jesus attempted to quiet him. He was creating a scene. They pushed him aside. They tried to discourage him. But the blind man continued in his effort. He shouted his prayer again and again, until an answer came.

Jesus asked the blind man, "What do you want Me to do for you?" The blind man replied, "Lord, make me see." Jesus said, "You shall see." And the man saw!

The blind man from Jericho knew his opportunity had come. His effort in seizing this opportunity was well rewarded. Suppose, however, he had said, "This Jesus can do nothing for me. I am blind!" Suppose he had been more interested in filling his pocketbook? Suppose he had not been so insistent upon making his way to Jesus?

You and I have the opportunity of seeing the priceless value of spiritual light. Yet many of us allow Jesus to pass us by, because we are too busy filling our pocketbooks, too busy enjoying worldly pleasures, too involved in earthly duties and concerns.

We need to be more like the blind man from Jericho. He approached Jesus in faith. He gave no thought to worldly gain. He paid no heed to those who tried to discourage him. He continued with his voice raised in prayer, "Lord, help me see!" He repeated his prayer until an answer came. He proved that those who diligently seek Jesus, will be given a light that overcomes their darkness.

Truly, we can learn much from the physically blind. A dear friend of mine was blind. Recently, God called him to his eternal home. This friend had been blind for nearly forty years. He lost his eyesight at the beginning of his manhood. People were moved to compassion at the sight of him. Yet, he saw more than many of them. He had seized his opportunity to approach Jesus.

My friend could not see the Words in the Holy Scriptures, but he could feel them with his hands. A day did not pass by in which he neglected his study of the Bible. He could not see the hymns or the liturgy we use at our worship services. But Sunday after Sunday, you would find him in church singing the hymns and taking part in the service from memory!

Night after night, he prayed, "Lord, help me see." Day after day, he used all the channels the Lord placed at his disposal to see. And he did see! He saw the wonders of the world far more beautiful than the one we see with our eyes.

My friends, no one wants to be blind. But many of us are. We are spiritually incapable of seeing that which is of vital significance. Each new day, Jesus approaches us. He inquires, "What will you have Me do for you?" Let us reply, "Lord, help us receive our spiritual sight."

With the help of the Holy Spirit, let us make a special effort to be persistent in our prayers, earnest in our devotions, and sincere in our study of God's Word. And we shall see the wonders of God's love. We shall see what God has done for us. We shall see what really counts.

<u>Prayer</u>:

Lord, we become so wrapped up in ourselves and what the world offers, we become blind and walk in darkness. We forget all flesh is as grass, and the glory of man is as the flower of grass. The grass withers and the flower falls away. Only Your Word endures forever. We pray You, therefore, to help us see those things which really count. Send us Your Holy Spirit. Direct us to Your Word, which was made flesh and dwelt among us — full of grace and truth. Make Jesus Christ a lamp unto our feet. Grant that we may daily follow Him, so we do not walk in darkness. As seed is sown in the ground, help us to implant His saving gospel within our hearts. Through Him, help us to behold the wonders of Your love. AMEN.

(For the continuation of this Prayer, see "PRAYER" on page 2 in the Suggestions segment)

<u>Hymn</u>: "Pass Me Not, O Gentle Savior"

Are You Getting the Results from Your Prayers?

Hymn: "Sweet Hour of Prayer"

Scripture Lesson: Matthew 7: 7-11

Sermon: "Are You Getting the Results from Your Prayers?"

It does not matter who you are, what you are, where you are. It matters not whether you are rich or poor; weak or strong; young or old. We all encounter needs passing through the wilderness of this life. We have all teetered upon the brink of despair.

You and I have longed for relief from a tormented soul; peace from a troubled spirit. We have yearned for strength in time of weakness — joy, in time of sorrow — guidance, in time of doubt — companionship, in time of loneliness.

And yet, whatever the need, the medication is ours for the asking! Prayer is the appointed way of obtaining a soothing salve. Prayer opens the treasure of Heavenly blessings. Prayer sets the fountain of Heaven's gifts flowing.

Unfortunately, when many of us do not obtain the riches we desire, we lose heart. If our thirst is not quenched immediately, we believe our prayers have been in vain. We wonder if God is deaf! We wonder if God cares!

In the 18th chapter of the Gospel of Saint Luke, Jesus tells a story urging us to be persistent in our prayers. He compels us to keep faith in God's love and mercy.

There are two characters in this story. One is an unrighteous judge who has no fear of God. He cares not for his fellow men.

The other is a poor, friendless, and helpless widow. She encounters great need. Someone is attempting to oppress her. The only one who can vindicate her from her adversary is the unrighteous judge. The widow approaches him. But he refuses to help her.

What is she to do? She has no money to bribe him. She has no friends to influence him. She has no power to bully him. She, therefore, does the only thing she can do. She continues to approach him. Day after day, night after night, she beseeches him. Finally, he can take no more! He says, "Although I care not for this woman, I will vindicate her, or her persistency will wear me out."

Jesus concludes His story, asking, "Now, if a hard-hearted, unrighteous judge will hear a persistent plea, then how much more will a Merciful and Loving God?"

The question before us is, "Are your prayers producing results?" If not, do not think for a moment God is deaf! Do not think He does not care. The problem lies in the way you are praying.

When many of us pray, we utter words and nothing more. We ask, but put little heart and soul into our asking. We knock, but our knocking does not reveal hunger and thirst. We seek, but do not persist until the answer is found.

To obtain results, we must pray with enduring faith in God's love and mercy. We must pray with a positive attitude, not a negative one. We must ask, knowing we will receive. We must knock, believing the door will be opened. We must seek, determined that we shall find.

If, after praying in this manner, the answer to our prayer appears delayed, we can be assured that it is for our own good. "Thy Will Be Done," not our will. God knows far better than you or I what is best for us.

My friends, whatever your need, pray! Pray without ceasing. Be likened unto the needy widow. Be persistent. Fight the good fight. Keep the faith!

<u>Prayer</u>:

Loving and merciful Father, the giver and sustainer of this life, we thank You for the blessing of prayer. You have taught us the importance of prayer by the example of Your Son. We therefore beseech You to help us, especially during our trials and tribulations, not to be anxious or fearful, but in everything by our persistent prayers and supplications, to make our needs known unto You. Fill us with Your Spirit and comforting presence.

Grant that we may come boldly unto the throne of Your grace. Give us faith to know that whatsoever we ask of You in the Name of Christ Jesus, with believing hearts, You will grant unto us according to Your Holy Will. Assure us You know better than we what is best for us. Help us always say, "Your will be done." AMEN.

(For the continuation of this Prayer, see "PRAYER" on page 2 in the Suggestions segment)

Hymn: "The Beautiful Garden of Prayer"

A Worthless Cistern or a Bubbling Spring?

Hymn: "My God, How Wonderful Thou Art"

Scripture Lesson: Deuteronomy 6: 4-25

Sermon: "A Worthless Cistern or a Bubbling Spring?"

Is there anyone taken more for granted than our Creator and Father in Heaven? Our response to His love — our forsaking Him in the manner which so many of us do — can and will only prove to be disastrous.

Perhaps the problem can best be summarized by way of the Old Testament Book of Jeremiah, chapter 2, Verse 13:

> "For My children have committed two evils:
>
> They have forsaken Me, the fountain of living water,
>
> And hewed out cisterns for themselves, broken cisterns that can hold no water."

During Jeremiah's time, as well as in many parts of the world today, where springs and wells are few, much reliance had to be placed upon cisterns. Cisterns are vessels that hold water from rain or other collection. Now at best, as you are probably aware, a cistern becomes an extremely poor substitute for a spring or well, because it contains mostly rainwater. Needless to say, when the cistern is cracked and the water oozes away, it becomes absolutely and utterly worthless.

Our text reveals a mystified prophet. Jeremiah is unable to comprehend how his people could possibly have forgotten all the Lord God had done for them. The Heavenly Father had delivered His children from their bondage in Egypt. He had lovingly and tenderly guided them across the treacherous wilderness. He had brought them into a rich and fertile land. Indeed, the Lord God had been good to His children.

But how were His children responding to this love? There were pushing the Lord God into the background. They were disobedient and unfaithful, allowing themselves to be dominated by the ways of the world. To make matters worse, they were worshiping other gods — false gods. Such gods are referred to as "baals" in the Old Testament.

These "baals" were man-made gods. Every village had its own "baal." Some were constructed out of wood, others out of stone, and still others out of metal. Some of these "baals" were the sun or moon, the trees or rivers. Some were nothing more than images in the minds of people.

These "baals" that the Israelites worshipped could be used or abused. They were impersonal gods — gods with no powers. As Jeremiah stated, "They are gods which are no gods."

Is it any wonder why Jeremiah was so mystified — why he could not comprehend how his people could forsake the giver of endless blessing for these "baals?" It seems ridiculous and absurd, doesn't it?

How could Israelites possibly forsake the Almighty God, the fountain of living water, in order to hew out cisterns for themselves —broken cisterns, which could hold no water?

Yet, how so very much we are to be likened unto these Israelites of long ago? In this 21st century, we are constantly forsaking the living fountain of water for worthless cisterns. We forsake the One True God, as revealed to us in the Person of Jesus Christ, to worship gods which are not gods.

The alcoholic makes alcohol his god. The drug addict makes drugs his god. The lustful individual makes lust and passion his god. There are many who make money and material possessions a god. There are those who make their profession a god. There are those who make worry and care, loneliness and self-pity, sorrow and grief a god.

The one God we have all worshipped is self. We are constantly placing entirely too much faith in ourselves, and not nearly enough in the Father in Heaven. For some unknown reason, we seem to prefer to manage our own lives. By so doing, we choose the uncertainty, the insecurity, and the dissatisfaction of a life lived without God -- without His guidance and grace. This way can only lead to a life of frustration, unhappiness, and anxiety.

I suppose we could go on and on, listing all the countless ways in which we forsake our Father in Heaven in order to worship all kinds of "baals."

My friends, if you had a choice between a spring which continuously bubbles over with clear, cool water, and a worthless cistern, there can be no doubt — you would naturally select the spring. You are fully aware that the water from the spring would supply your every need.

The question which disturbed Jeremiah was "*why?*" Why do my people forsake the Lord God, the Almighty God, the God of Love and Justice Who has done and will do so much for them — the God Who can enrich their lives with endless eternal blessings — for their worthless "baals?"

Why do we do the same today?

> "For my children have committed two evils:
>
> They have forsaken Me, the fountain of living water,
>
> And hewed out cisterns for themselves -- broken cisterns that can hold no water."

Which will it be in your life — a worthless cistern, or a bubbling spring?

Prayer:

O merciful and loving Shepherd, Who is the eternal spring of bubbling blessings, enable us to see that we need dread nothing but the loss of You. Help us each day to rely only upon You, and to realize all other gods are worthless and can only flood our lives with frustration and anxiety, unhappiness and hopelessness. Only You can lead us to green pastures and beside the still waters. Fill us with Your Holy Spirit so we may always feel Your nearness, and have the assurance You will support our weakness; increase our strength; and satisfy all our needs. AMEN.

Hymn: "A Mighty Fortress Is Our God"

The Highway to Heaven

Hymn: "Thou, Whose Almighty Word"

Scripture Lesson: John 10: 7-10, Revelation 21: 1-4

Sermon: "The Highway to Heaven"

Human life is nothing more than a journey — a journey to the grave! The life of the believer is also a journey, but a journey to a new world.

In the 35th chapter of Isaiah, the prophet paints a vivid picture of what we can expect when our present journey ends. He tells us that at the end of time, two outstanding events will occur. There will be vengeance and punishment for the wicked. There will be redemption for the faithful.

When the end comes, there will be a manifestation of the Almighty God in all His power and glory, as Deliverer. The redeemed shall be full of song, for they shall inherit eternal joy and gladness. Sorrow, pain, and sighing shall pass away.

To become part of this great transformation, Isaiah informs us we must now travel the Holy Way. We must now travel the route known as the Lord's Highway. This road will take us directly to the Heavenly Father — to all He is eternally prepared to give us out of His love.

We began our journey along the Lord's Highway when we were baptized. When we were confirmed, we were also on His Highway.

But are you still traveling this road? Or have you been led astray? It is so easy to make the wrong turn upon reaching a fork in the road. It is so easy to take the wrong exit.

Who among us has not experienced making the wrong turn, or taking the wrong exit? We began our journey on the right highway, but somewhere along the road, we were misled. Perhaps we were not alert to the signs along our route. Perhaps someone gave us the wrong directions.

In any case, as soon as we became aware of our error, we made every effort to correct it. We made every attempt to locate the highway which would take us to our destination.

Are you still on the Lord's Highway? The route is clearly marked by way of God's Word as revealed to us in the Holy Scriptures — by way of the Lord Jesus Christ.

Are you following the directions given to us? It appears many of us are not.

We are told to love — yet, we envy, hate, and are critical.

We are told to forgive — yet, we hold grudges.

We are told to bear one another's burdens — yet, we think only of ourselves.

We are told to believe – yet, we doubt.

We are told to witness to others of God's Love — yet, we ignore our un-churched neighbor.

We are told to be patient — yet, we lack understanding.

We are told to cast our burdens upon the Lord — yet, we cling to our anxieties; we cling to our problems and afflictions.

Need we continue? The guideposts which God supplies direct us to do one thing — yet, we do another.

As long as we neglect our Bibles, as long as we ignore the teachings of Christ Jesus, how can we say we are walking on the Lord's Highway?

But the Loving Father in Heaven never ceases His search for those who have wandered astray. Through His Holy Word; through His Holy Spirit; through the Word of His Church; through those who witness for Him, He continues to help us find our way. Through the life, through the love and victory of Jesus Christ, He makes it possible for everyone to travel along His Highway.

My friends, there are many roads in this life. But there is only one that will take us home to God.

Hear the Lord Jesus Christ as He calls to you — as He calls to me. "This is the Way, walk ye in it."

It is not a dead-end street! It is a road which will take you to a transformed Kingdom.

> "A Kingdom where the weak shall be made strong
>
> -- Where the fearful shall be made courageous
>
> -- Where the eyes of the blind shall be opened
>
> -- Where the ears of the deaf shall be unstopped
>
> -- Where the lame and crippled shall leap like a hart
>
> -- Where the tongue of the dumb shall sing for joy
>
> -- Where there shall be streams in the desert
>
> -- Where all shall obtain joy and gladness
>
> -- Where sorrow, pain and sighing shall pass away."

Prayer:

Heavenly Father, the author and Creator, giver and sustainer of life, we pray You to forgive us for the endless times we have wandered from Your Highway. Forgive us for being deaf to Your Voice; for having driven You away by willful selfishness, denial, and disloyalty. We pray You to fill us with Your Holy Spirit. Enlighten our hearts in the Way and Truth revealed unto us by Your Son Jesus Christ. Give us an unshakable faith in Him.

Whatever our adversity, grant that our faith will give us the victory which overcomes the world. Make us partakers of the life He promises to those who love and trust Him. Grant that we may be with You for evermore in Your Transformed Kingdom, where we shall inherit eternal joy and gladness — where sorrow, pain, and sighing shall pass away. AMEN.

(For the continuation of this Prayer, see "PRAYER" on page 2 in the Suggestions segment)

Hymn: "I Am Thine, O Lord"

A Golden Age for God's Children

<u>Hymn</u>: "How Great Thou Art"

<u>Scripture Lesson</u>: Revelation 7: 9-17

<u>Sermon</u>: "A Golden Age for God's Children"

On All Saints' Sunday, we commemorate those who have died in the faith. We commemorate all the saints who have passed from this life to the next.

A saint is a forgiven sinner, a sinner who through his or her faith in the Lord Jesus Christ has become justified in the sight of God.

In the New Testament Book of Hebrews, we are told:

> "There exists a full and complete Rest for the children of God. He that now experiences this Glorious Rest is resting from his labors."
>
> "But let us who still labor, be eager to know this Rest for ourselves. Let us be cautious that we do not miss this wondrous Rest, by falling into unbelief and disobedience. Let us remember — God knows the thoughts and motives in our hearts. Let us remember — we cannot hide anything from His sight. Everything stands naked and exposed before His eyes."

There are two parts to this text.

The first part speaks of those who have died in the faith. They are now resting from their labors. They are partakers of the "Golden Age." They are enjoying "Paradise." They now experience complete freedom from pain and sorrow, trial and tribulation. They have peace. They are eternally free from the clutches of the devil and sin — death and the grave.

They now dwell in the heavenly Mansion that Jesus Christ has prepared for all who love Him. They shall hunger no more. Neither shall they thirst. Blessed indeed are the dead, which die in the Lord.

Whereas the first part of our text speaks of those who died in the faith, the second part speaks of those living in the faith.

We who still labor should be eager to also know the Heavenly Rest which the departed saints now enjoy. But we must be cautious or else, by way of our unbelief and disobedience, we forfeit the "Golden Age" which awaits the faithful. Do not be foolish. Remember, the Heavenly Father knows the thoughts and motives in your hearts. You are not able to hide anything from His sight. Everything you think or say or do, stands naked and exposed before His eyes.

My friends, as you can see, we need not be concerned about those who have died in the faith. But we do need to be concerned about whether or not we are living in the faith.

Come to Jesus with repentant and believing hearts. Receive forgiveness for your failures and shortcomings. Experience the peace which awaits all who live in Jesus Christ.

Prayer:

Lord God, we remember with heartfelt gratitude those who have loved and served You on earth, who now rest from their labors (especially those most dear to us whom we name in our hearts before You).

Lord, we know not the day or the hour. We beseech You to help us work Your Works while it is day, before the night comes when no man can work. You gave us Jesus that in and through Him, we have knowledge of the Way and Truth, which enables us to have the life that knows no ending. Faith in Jesus allows us to dwell in the Heavenly mansion where all the Saints who have departed from this life now dwell. They no longer experience sorrow or crying; pain or suffering; trial or tribulation. They only experience peace which passes all human understanding. Truly, they live in the "Golden Age."

Lord, flood our beings with the Holy Spirit. Each new day fill our hearts with faith in the One Who said, "He that believeth in Me, though he were dead, yet shall he live; and whosoever liveth and believeth in Me shall never die."

(For the continuation of this Prayer, see "PRAYER" on page 2 in the Suggestions segment)

Hymn: "Beautiful Isle of Somewhere"

How Do You Look?

Hymn: "Blest Are the Pure in Heart"

Scripture Lesson: Matthew 23: 25-28

Sermon: "How Do You Look?"

On many occasions, whenever the opportunity has presented itself, we have asked a loved one how we look. How pleased we were upon receiving his or her approval.

That we humans are extremely concerned regarding our outward appearance is revealed by the fact that we disburse endless time and millions of dollars each year for this purpose. And in the process of doing so, many of us unfortunately lose sight of the truth that although a book might have an attractive cover, its content may be ugly and dreadful. We cannot deny that being well groomed is important. But which is more important — the cover, or the content of a book? If only we cared for our interiors with the same devotion we employ for caring for our exteriors!

What does the Bible say concerning this matter? In the 16th chapter of the Old Testament Book of 1 Samuel, we are told that Samuel had been commissioned by the Lord God to anoint a successor to King Saul. To accomplish this mission, Samuel had invited a man from Bethlehem called Jesse, along with his sons, to join him.

The seven sons of Jesse standing before Samuel were certainly a sight to behold. They were handsome, tall and muscular, mature men possessing desirable personalities. By our standards, any one of Jesse's sons would have made an impressive-looking king — would easily have become a 21st century idol.

Samuel carefully studied the seven young men, and then selected the one which appeared to outshine the other six. Samuel said, "Surely the Lord's anointed now stands before me. Surely this is the one who shall be the new King of Israel."

But the Lord said to Samuel, "Do not look upon his appearance or upon the height of his stature, because I have rejected him. I see not as man sees. Man looks upon the outward appearance, but I look into the heart."

Samuel then requested that the other six sons again stand before him. After closely overseeing each one, Samuel remarked, "The Lord has not chosen any of these."

Then Samuel turned to Jesse and inquired, "Are all your sons present?" Jesse replied, "They are all here but David, who is presently caring for my sheep, but he is young and not yet mature in mind or stature." Samuel commanded Jesse to send for David. When the youth appeared, the Lord said to Samuel, "Arise, anoint him, for this is he."

Although David's brothers surpassed him in maturity and physical stature, he was selected to be the next King of Israel. David was qualified for this position because he possessed a tender and gentle, kind and sympathetic nature. This was revealed by the way he provided for his father's sheep. He conscientiously sought after the welfare of each animal in the flock. He gave special attention to the needy — the sick and crippled. Surely, one who cared for his earthly father's flock in the manner David did, would care much more for the flock belonging to his Heavenly Father.

As Christians, our estimation of ourselves and others cannot be founded upon outward manifestations — upon the way we dress and the way our hair looks.

We human beings are constantly erring in our judgments concerning ourselves and our fellow men, simply because so many of us stop at the surface. We forget that external beauty is no guarantee of internal worth. Unfortunately, our false judgments create untold damage and suffering.

The Lord God does not err in His judgments regarding us, because He penetrates the cover. He looks into the hidden depths of the soul and sees the exact conditions that exist. He knows why we do, or do not communicate with Him daily — why we do, or do not make the kind of contributions to His Kingdom He desires — why we do, or do not treat all our brethren with heartfelt compassion.

My friends, although we may impress others with our outward appearances and performances, we may not impress the Heavenly Father.

Therefore, be sure that your heart is right. Be certain you have the heart of Jesus Christ. As David won favor in the sight of God, so can we do likewise if we permit the Master and Savior to show us the Way.

And the Lord said to Samuel, "Do not look upon his appearance or upon the height of his stature, because I have rejected him. I see not as man sees. Man looks upon the outward appearance, but I look into the heart."

How do you look? Are you satisfied with what you see? But more important, *do you believe God is satisfied with what He sees*?

Prayer:

Oh Lord God, Who sees not as man sees, but Who looks into the heart, help us to see that how we look outwardly is really unimportant. Help us to always focus our minds upon that which is truly vital. Do not permit the things of this world to rob us of a true sense of value. Fill us with Your Holy Spirit. Flood us with holy desires. Guide and direct us, that we may nourish whatever will enable us to lead godly lives. So possess our hearts that our thoughts and speech and acts permit us to live in such a manner, that all about us may know and see You and desire to be Yours. May our hearts always reflect such trust and obedience, fear and love for You, so we may in the end receive what You have promised to us through Jesus Christ, our Lord and Savior. AMEN.

(For the continuation of this Prayer, see "PRAYER" on page 2 in the Suggestions segment)

Hymn: "Take My Life, and Let It Be"

Will You Reject This Invitation?

Hymn: "There Is a Wideness in God's Mercy"

Scripture Lesson: John 6: 35-40

Sermon: "Will You Reject This Invitation?"

In the deserts of Central Australia, there is a strange plant closely associated with the fern family. I have been told that a group of English explorers, while crossing these deserts, were compelled to depend upon this plant as their major source of food. The plant satisfied their hunger.

Yet, day after day, these men became weaker and weaker. Their flesh literally wasted away. Their strength became so reduced; they could travel only a short distance at a time. One by one they began to perish. Only one survivor remained when located by a rescue party.

It was discovered that these poor, unfortunate men had died of starvation. When analyzed, the plant which they had depended upon to sustain them was found to lack adequate nutritious elements.

This story vividly illustrates what is happening to man today. As human beings, we possess countless needs. We suffer from guilt and loneliness, worry and despair, pain and torment; the list of our needs is an endless one.

We attempt to satisfy these needs. But we do so with the food this world offers. We nail our hopes upon material possessions and pleasures, alcohol and drugs, and upon whatever else we can obtain from this world.

Unfortunately, we fail to realize that although this so-called worldly food may temporarily satisfy us, such satisfaction is brief in duration. If we continue to depend upon such earthy nourishment, we shall surely perish.

Only the Almighty God can supply what is needful for the suffering, afflicted, and sinful man.

Let us direct our attention to the 55th chapter of Isaiah, verses 1-7.

> The prophet Isaiah says to his people, "Why do you spend your money for that which is not bread? Why do you spend your labor for that which does not satisfy? Why do you devote your time and energies to those things which will only destroy? Come! Come to the Lord God! Hear what He has to say to you, so that your soul might live! He will make with you an everlasting covenant."

Isaiah is looking into the future. The covenant of which the prophet speaks is the one that God the Father has established through Jesus Christ.

God has made Jesus a witness to His people. Through Christ, man can come to know his Creator.

God has made Jesus a leader and Shepherd. Through Christ, man will be cared for and led to the path of righteousness. Man will find favor in his Creator's sight.

God has made Jesus a commander. Through Christ, man shall be led to victory over his enemies and foes.

Through the Lord Jesus Christ, the Almighty God has made provision for every human need.

So come! Come to the Lord and Master! Come to the Savior of mankind. By so doing, you will come to your Creator and Father in Heaven.

He who hungers and thirsts, come eat and drink. Come and be replenished, without money and without price.

These Words are an invitation from Heaven to you. They bid you to come to the Almighty God through Jesus Christ. Whatever your need, whatever your hunger and thirst; come and receive your Heavenly Father's Divine Grace. Satisfy your hunger with His blessings of pardon and salvation. Satisfy your thirst with His refreshing waters.

Let no one say the Lord God is not concerned about His suffering children. He cares deeply for the afflicted and heavily laden. The rich cannot buy the Heavenly Father's Grace, nor is the poorest of men kept back by his poverty. What God gives is free.

We all have needs. Therefore, with the Help of the Holy Spirit, should we not accept this gracious invitation?

But come now! For you and I must seek the Lord while He may be found! We must call upon Him while He is near. If we do not seek or call upon the Lord in this life, we certainly cannot expect to seek or call upon Him in the next.

Many of us are walking in the wrong direction. God bids us to turn back. Now is the time to change directions!

My friends, the English explorers spent their time and energies feeding upon an earthly plant which appeared to sustain their needs. But for one exception, they all perished. Let us not make the same mistake! Let us not depend upon the things of this world, which are brief in duration and do not truly sustain.

Only the loving Heavenly Father can truly provide. Therefore, let us not live our lives apart from Him. Let us abundantly eat and drink of the blessings which only He can supply.

The terms for these blessings are within reach of us all. Simply stretch your arms heavenward with believing hearts.

You and I must nail our hopes upon the Lord Jesus Christ. God will do the rest.

<u>Prayer</u>:

Lord God, Our Father in Heaven, Who through the Work of Your Spirit is ever inviting us to come unto You, we pray You to show us the folly of our dependency upon the things of this world. Guide and direct us to Your Son Jesus Christ, the Shepherd and Savior of us all. Grant us unwavering faith in Him. Through Him, help us live in constant and closest union with You. Help us to safely pass through the perils we encounter in this life, by feeding our famished souls with Your Heavenly bread. Grant we may always feel the sure comfort of Your love and mercy. Satisfy our thirst. Sustain our needs, whatever they may be. AMEN.

(For the continuation of this Prayer, see "PRAYER" on page 2 in the Suggestions segment)

Hymn: "God Will Take Care of You"

Sour Notes

Hymn: "Blest Be the Tie That Binds"

Scripture Lesson: Genesis 13: 8, Matthew 5: 21-24

Sermon: "Sour Notes"

Some time ago, I read about a young woman who committed suicide. She left behind the following note: "I experience nothing but discord. I long for harmony. Perhaps I shall find it where I am now going."

This young woman represents only one life — one out of billions. Fortunately, the majority of people encountering her problem of conflict do not attempt to find a solution to their misery and unhappiness by self-destruction. Needless to say, the young woman acted impulsively. But her act of desperation vividly conveys the seriousness of the problem. And the problem is certainly not a new one. From the beginning of time, man has been compelled to associate with other human beings. And whenever there is discord in these human relationships, the end result is almost always anxiety in one form or another.

In the 12th chapter of Romans, verses 9-12, the Apostle Paul implores us to "live in harmony." If only you and I would permit this simple and short sentence to play a prominent role within our lives, what a wondrous contribution we could make to the human race.

Let us briefly consider what is involved, pertaining to living in harmony. The term harmony was derived from a Greek word meaning "concord." It implies agreement and union, unison and unity.

When employing the term harmony, is it not true, many of us direct our thoughts to music? We relate the term to an a cappella group, a barber-shop quartette, or a choir. Therefore, it might be to our advantage to consider harmony as it is applied to music, in order to come to a better understanding as to how it ought to be applied to human relationships.

To produce harmony, the first major step for any choral group is to work upon the same foundation. All within the group must concentrate their efforts upon the same musical selection.

Although a choral group may consist of many individuals, it is divided into various sections singing different musical parts. The objective of each section is the blending of their voices with the others. Harmony results when agreement between and among the various musical parts is created. However, one sour note will quickly mar or shatter the harmony.

What is true regarding harmony in music is also true concerning harmony among human beings. If you and I hope to obtain unity, we must work upon the same foundation. We must have the same goal. As Saint Paul states, "We must have the same mind of our Lord and Savior, Jesus Christ."

We must also bear in mind that no two human beings are alike. We possess different moods and desires, ideas and roles. Therefore, to create union and agreement, it becomes necessary to make allowances for one another.

In other words, if we have the same "mind of Christ Jesus," and at the same time make every effort to blend our differences, the end result will most certainly be a relationship of beauty.

But self-centeredness and worldliness, bitterness and prejudice, malice and gossip, bad tempers and manners can be the sour notes which can injure or destroy this relationship.

How desperately our present world yearns for the harmony of which we speak. How disturbing it becomes to observe a lack of agreement among those of us who confess to be Christians — who profess to have the same "mind of Jesus Christ."

In fact, how can you and I ever hope to preach harmony among our fellow men, if we do not strive for harmony among ourselves and those we encounter during the course of a single day? Are you daily practicing the teaching of the Apostle Paul? What are you doing in your life to nourish the "plant of harmony?"

Paul suggests that we bless those who curse us — we do not return evil for evil — we do not become set in our opinions — we take a sincere and active interest in every human being, regardless of his social rank – we love one another with brotherly affection — we share the happiness of those who are happy, and the sorrow of those who are sorrowful — we give freely to others in time of need — we live in peace with everyone.

He further urges us to endure our trials and tribulations patiently, remembering at all times that the Father in Heaven is our refuge and strength, a very present help in time of trouble. Avoid, if possible, compelling another to carry the cross assigned to you. Rather, rejoice in your hope. Be aglow with the Holy Spirit. Be constant in prayer.

There are so many ways in which we can supply the "plant of harmony" with the nourishment it requires to survive in a sin-enslaved world. It cannot be denied that, inasmuch as no two human beings are exactly alike, it will become extremely difficult at times to nourish this harmony plant. But for the sake of Christ Jesus, you and I must practice blending our differences, the same as a four- or eight-part choral group practices to blend their voices in order to obtain harmony.

My friends, remember it only takes one sour note to create discord — to destroy the beauty of any musical selection. In your relationship with others, do not be a sour note. Let us do as Saint Paul implores. Let us live in harmony.

Prayer:

Father in Heaven, fill us with Your Grace so we might at all times be prevented from being sour notes in our human relationships. Give us the same "mind of Christ Jesus." May we love one another as He has loved us. Help us to blend our differences and to live in harmony. Help us to be compassionate and understanding, possessing sweet and gentle dispositions. Help us when wronged by others, not to render evil for evil nor insult for insult, but to bend and return good. As Your children, may our attitude towards others please and glorify You. AMEN.

(For the continuation of this Prayer, see "PRAYER" on page 2 in the Suggestions segment)

Hymn: "In Christ There Is No East or West"

What a Friend We Have in Jesus

Hymn: "How Sweet the Name of Jesus Sounds"

Scripture Lesson: 1 Peter 5: 6-11

Sermon: "What a Friend We Have in Jesus"

One of the major problems confronting the human being in this 21st century is fear. In our conflict with opponents of this life, we on many occasions experience a terrifying and paralyzing fear creeping into our hearts and minds. But why; why do we permit ourselves to become so afraid of the enemy?

It is said a small girl came limping home. "What happened?" inquired the father. The answer: "Some of the bigger girls tried to make me do something I knew was wrong. When I told them I would not do what they wanted, they pushed me. I fell and hit my knee on a stone."

"Weren't you afraid?" asked the father. The reply was: "No, because I knew my friend Jesus was with me and would help me, if I needed Him."

If only you and I would allow the Holy Spirit to give us the faith of this little girl. If only you and I would believe in the Lord Jesus Christ — trust and love Him in this child-like manner — fear would never dominate our lives.

For example, are you afraid of death?

Doesn't Jesus tell us, "in His Father's Home there are many mansions, and that He has gone there to prepare a place for those who love Him?"

Doesn't He also tell us, "He is the Resurrection and the Life, and that whosoever believes in Him, though he were dead, yet shall he live, and whosoever lives and believes in Him, shall never die?"

Are you afraid of the consequences of your sins?

Doesn't Jesus tell us, "He came to seek and to save the lost ... that He is the new covenant between you and God ... that He willingly gave His Body and shed His Blood, for the remission of your sins?"

Are you afraid of being alone?

Doesn't Jesus tell us, "He will be with you always, even unto the end of this present age?"

Are you afraid of trial and tribulation, affliction and suffering, pain and despair?

Doesn't Jesus tell us, "We should not let our hearts be troubled ... that we should cast our cares upon Him, knowing He cares for us ... that we should come unto Him with our burdens so He can give us rest?"

Are you concerned about what you are going to eat or drink; about what you are going to wear? Exactly what are your fears?

Doesn't Jesus tell us, "We should not be anxious about this present life? Look at the birds of the air. They neither sow nor reap nor gather into barns. Yet, the Heavenly Father and Creator provides for them. Certainly you are of much more value than they, you men of little faith. Your Father in Heaven knows what your needs are. If you seek His Kingdom first, He will truly fulfill your every need."

Perhaps one of the major reasons why so many of us experience various forms of fear creeping into our hearts and minds, is that we place too little value upon the Kingdom of which Jesus speaks, and too much value upon the kingdoms of this world.

My friends, whatever your fears may be, trust the Lord and Savior to sustain you. God the Father will indeed provide through Him. Why permit yourselves to become so afraid of the enemies of this life?

All you must do is believe in Jesus Christ. He is the dearest and truest friend you have.

<u>Prayer</u>:

Merciful and Loving Father, we laud and magnify Your Glorious Name for the countless and wondrous blessings we so abundantly receive through Your Son, Jesus Christ. Whenever we experience crushing doubts and paralyzing fears, or whenever any danger threatens or assails our physical, mental, and spiritual health, we implore You to fill us with Your Holy Spirit. Enable us to know we are not alone. Direct us to Jesus. Give us the assurance He will sustain our every need and deliver us from our every foe. Grant we will always see Him as the dearest and truest friend we have. Permit His Gospel and promises to drive away our shadows of despair, and to heal our every woe. AMEN.

(For the continuation of this Prayer, see "PRAYER" on page 2 in the Suggestions segment)

Hymn: "O Love That Wilt Not Let Me Go"

Keep the Fire Burning

Hymn: "Lead, Kindly Light"

Scripture Lesson: 1 Corinthians 10: 31-11: 1

Sermon: "Keep the Fire Burning"

In the 12th chapter of Romans, verses 11-12, Saint Paul tells us, "Never flag in zeal, be aglow with the Spirit, serve the Lord. Rejoice in your hope, be patient in tribulation, be constant in prayer."

"Never flag in zeal, be aglow with the Spirit, serve the Lord."

The responsibilities of the Christian are many. Although you and I possess different gifts and play various roles in this life, we should be very busy serving the Lord in whatever manner we can. All we do should be done with one goal in mind — making His Way and Truth live within this world.

We need to be reminded that Christianity is found in what we do and say and think. Christianity involves the total life. As followers of Jesus, we must radiate in all directions. God-ward and man-ward; Heaven-ward and earth-ward.

Serving the Lord is a full-time job. There is no room for halfhearted-ness or lukewarm-ness. Slackness can destroy our effectiveness as the Lord's instruments. To serve the Lord effectively, it is essential to keep the fire of God's presence burning within us. To maintain this spiritual glow in our lives, we must constantly feed upon the proper fuel.

Life is not the candle or the wick. It is the burning. Only when the candle is producing light and heat, is it effectively serving its purpose.

We know how difficult it is for a candle to maintain its glow in the wind or rain. How equally difficult it is for us for us to maintain our spiritual glow, when enthusiasm give way to disillusionment.

As you know, life is not always a bed of roses. Life is full of ups and downs. We live, and yet many things happen which we do not understand.

Questions arise to which we cannot find the answers. Bright dreams become harsh realities. Hope fades into bitterness.

Amid the hard knocks which come our way, it is vitally important that we maintain our spiritual flame. When our spiritual glow flickers and burns low, we must labor all the more to obtain the appropriate fuel. If we do not, we run the risk of our flame going out. When the glow, which a *living faith* brings to life, diminishes, a baffled sense of futility creeps into the heart. This is exactly what is happening to so many individuals living in today's world.

Far too many personalities are feasting upon the fuel furnished by "Satan's Fuel Company." They are attempting to satisfy their hunger and thirst with the things of this world. Is it any wonder their spiritual flames are not being quenched? Is it any wonder there is so much hopelessness and discouragement, fear and despair, self-concern and self-pity — any wonder why endless anxieties engulf the 21st century man?

Anyone who thinks his spiritual life will take care of itself is making a grave mistake. As the flame of a candle requires the wick, so do we require the fuel which only God can provide.

We must constantly feed upon His Word. A Christian without the Living Word is a person without the glow. We must fight the temptations which prevent us from daily meditating upon His Word. We should look forward to reading our Bibles with the same eager anticipation we possess for our favorite television programs.

We should be in constant communication with God through our prayers. In this day and age, we need to communicate with Him more than ever before. The power of prayer can do a great deal for our spiritual life.

As ivy clings to a wall, so must you and I cling to the Lord Jesus Christ. Through the Work of the Holy Spirit, He will preserve and sustain us. His promises of present blessings and of future glories will give us much fuel to consume.

Christians should be people of fire. Our sole ambition should be to blaze, to give light and heat. To do that for which we have been called, we must be consuming energy possessed from within. To create this energy, we must depend upon the fuel given us by the Holy Spirit.

Only vigorous plants can survive earth's severe winters. Only vigorous Christians can survive the rigors of time.

Christians who keep their spiritual fires burning are protected against the withering blast of earth's storms. They are able to outlive the unfavorable influences which often surround them.

Christians who are aglow with the Spirit of God recover from the blows of life. They hear the music of the Lord's clear call, and serve Him at all times in whatever way they can.

My friends, "Never flag in zeal, be aglow with the Spirit, serve the Lord. Rejoice in your hope, be patient in tribulation, be constant in prayer."

Prayer:

Lord God, You know the earthly storms we encounter. We humbly thank You for the promises and the hope You give us through Your Son, Jesus Christ. Grant that His Saving Gospel may always be the fuel which sustains us. Fill us with Your Holy Spirit, so the light He gives in time of darkness may supply our every need. May His light not only shine within us, but through us. May no hardship or fear, danger or distress, deter us from living our lives to Your Glory. Whatever our affliction or burden, help us to never flag in zeal; to be aglow with the Spirit; and to serve You at all times in whatever way we can. AMEN.

(For the continuation of this Prayer, see "PRAYER" on page 2 in the Suggestions segment)

Hymn: "I Love to Tell the Story"

Our Ship Has Docked

Hymn: "I Heard the Voice of Jesus"

Scripture Lesson: Romans 8: 31-39

Sermon: "Our Ship Has Docked"

Who among us has not experienced human misery and anxiety in one form or another? Is there a human being who has not suffered from fear or worry, pain or affliction, heartache or loneliness, despair or guilt? Indeed, we are well acquainted with the fact that life can become a terrifying nightmare, and darker than the darkest of nights.

The question is: How can we cope with these miseries and anxieties which so quickly saturate our lives?

If only our ship would come into port. If only the day would come whereby we could possess the means and resources to surmount.

Not only has our ship entered port, it has docked. And it is loaded with priceless treasures. The loving and merciful Father in Heaven has provided in abundance the necessary resources required to overcome. "Eye hath not seen, nor ear hath not heard — neither hath there entered the heart of man, the wondrous things which God hath prepared for them that truly love Him."

But if God has supplied us with the means to conquer, why do we then continue to wrestle and struggle with life's problems? Could it be because we are not making an honest and sincere effort to obtain this wealth which is ours for the asking?

To the best of my knowledge, the only way we can reach the other side of the street is to make an effort to cross. The same applies to the precious treasure which God is prepared to give us. If this wealth is to provide for and fulfill our countless needs, we must make a sincere effort to use these resources.

Unfortunately, many of us do not make this effort. Therefore, countless men and women in this 21st century continue to suffer needlessly.

For example, how many days have passed since you last studied your Bible? When was the last time you talked with God about the cares and burdens flooding your heart?

How often have you withdrawn to a quiet place for the purpose of real, soul-stirring meditation? Need we continue?

We possess vast resources which have not as yet been explored. We hesitate to make these explorations because of our love for the things of this world, and our cravings to satisfy the desires of the flesh. Our hesitation only enables us to scratch the surface, and prevents us from knowing how rich we really are. Our concern for self and egotistic ways prohibits us from availing ourselves of the spiritual capital which is ours to use.

The Apostle Paul made use of this spiritual capital. Consider the transformation which took place in his life. At one time, Paul had been a man of the world — had played a vital role in the movement attempting to crush and destroy Christianity. He had been a lost creature. But he struck it rich, simply by making a sincere effort to obtain the great wealth the Heavenly Father placed at his disposal.

Now with joy in his heart, fully aware of what God's love and grace can do for man, Paul writes these words in the 1st chapter of I Corinthians to his Christian brethren in Corinth:

> "I am always thanking God for you. I thank Him for His Grace given to you in Christ Jesus. I thank Him for all the enrichment that has come to you in Christ. You possess full knowledge and you can give full expression to it, because in you the evidence for the truth of Christ has found confirmation. You indeed lack no single gift, while you wait expectantly for our Lord Jesus Christ to reveal Himself. He will keep you firm to the end, without reproach on the Day of our Lord Jesus. It is God himself who called you to share in the life of His Son Jesus Christ our Lord."

Truly, these are words of congratulation to a people who had come into a great fortune — who had become heirs of God's love and grace, simply because they had accepted Jesus Christ as their Lord and Savior. Anyone who receives the love and grace of God through Christ Jesus and the Work of the Holy Spirit has wealth in abundance. And the more the individual concentrates upon receiving this love and grace, the richer he will become.

The Lord Jesus Christ marks the beginning of obtaining this glorious wealth of which we speak. He is Savior and Master, revealer and example. He is the Way, the Truth, and the Life. Once the testimony of His Gospel establishes the Heavenly Father's purpose in us, our lives shall indeed be enriched and blessed.

My friends, we no longer need to dream about the day our ship will enter port. It has docked. And it is loaded with incredible blessing and wealth. But of what benefit are these resources — how can they possible provide for any of our needs, if we do not make a sincere effort to receive and accept, employ and use them?

Prayer:

O Loving Father in Heaven, help us not to be so concerned with ourselves and the things of this world that we see not the precious cargo of treasures which You have prepared to give us. Through the Work of Your Holy Spirit, enable Your Son, Jesus Christ, who is the light of life and our only refuge and defense against the enemy, to dwell within our hearts. Encourage us to drink deeply from His Gospel and permit His countless promises to calm our troubled souls, and overcome the shadows and darkness which hover over our lives. Enable us to experience the wondrous and glorious transformation which the Apostle Paul and Your countless other children have experienced. In Jesus, Who makes it possible for everyone who believed in Him, help us rise above all worldly turmoil. AMEN.

(For the continuation of this Prayer, see "PRAYER" on page 2 in the Suggestions segment)

Hymn: "Jesus, Lover of My Soul"

Glory Not in Yourself, but in the Lord

Hymn: "How Great Thou Art"

Scripture Lesson: Genesis 1: 1-31

Sermon: "Glory Not in Yourself, but in the Lord"

One of the major problems confronting humanity today is boasting about our own achievements. We fail to realize that the more we boast, the more we rely upon our own resources. The more we rely upon our own resources, the more self-centered we become. And when we become too self-centered, we are in trouble. Self-glory can only lead to a fall.

Boasting is not new. Men have boasted of themselves for thousands of years. The Holy Scriptures do not tell us 'not' to boast! They simply caution us as to how.

In the 9th chapter of Jeremiah, we are told, "Let not the wise man glory in his wisdom. Let not the mighty man glory in his might. Let not the rich man glory in his riches. But, let him who glories, glory in the Lord."

"Let not the wise man glory in his wisdom." In our opinion, men may have great wisdom. We may know how to send a man into outer space; how to break the atom; how to transplant vital organs of the human body. But is there any real comparison between an anthill and a mountain? Can our wisdom be likened unto the wisdom of God? Regardless of how much wisdom we think we possess, we are like children playing on the seashore, with an ocean of wisdom before us. Our wisdom will take us only so far. Only God can supply us with the wisdom necessary for our well-being.

"Let not the mighty man glory in his might." Men may be able to dominate other men — lift two hundred pounds over their heads, break boards with a karate stroke — yet, by ourselves, we cannot overpower the devil and sin, death and the grave. The power we possess is insignificant compared with the omnipotence of Almighty God. We are frail, weak, and temporary, whereas God is strong. His strength endures. Only He can supply us with the might necessary for our well-being.

"Let not the rich man glory in his riches." Men may be able to double or triple their investments, accrue millions of dollars in profits, but have you ever been introduced to anyone who could buy his way into Heaven? Men cannot buy love or peace, true friends or loyalty, justice or righteousness. Only God can supply us with the riches necessary for our well-being.

With God, we are likened unto water being directed to turn the mighty mill.

Without God, we are compared to water breaking through its banks. We are desolate and destructive.

How foolhardy it is to boast about ourselves. Our boasting does not please God, and we are making a serious mistake if we think others enjoy listening to it.

What we can achieve by ourselves is not worth mentioning. But, what God achieves through us is! Therefore, if we must boast, let it be about God. He is the giver. Anything we possess worth bragging about, has been given to us by Him in the first place. Let us give credit where credit is due.

My friends, making a great noise about ourselves is ridiculous.

Let him who glories, glory in the Lord!

Prayer:

Lord God, of Whom — and through Whom — and to Whom are all things. We are Yours. We are Your children -- the sheep of Your pasture. You are our Creator and Sustainer. We beseech You; help us take heed so we do not fall. Help us see that when we glory in ourselves, we are likened unto clouds and wind without rain. You are the giver of all good and perfect gifts. You and You alone hold all things in the hollow of Your hand. Therefore, grant we trust not in our wisdom, might, and riches. Rather, help us always bow before You. Help us glorify Your Name, for the manifold blessings we enjoy. AMEN.

(For the continuation of this Prayer, see "PRAYER" on page 2 in the Suggestions segment)

Hymn: "O Worship the King"

The Night of Nights

Hymn: "I Am so Glad Each Christmas Eve"

Scripture Lesson: Luke 2: 8-20

Sermon: "The Nights of Nights"

Tonight is a night of mystery. It is a night of great expectation. It is a night likened unto one of long ago.

Near the town of Bethlehem, shepherds were watching their flocks. The sky was clear. The air — refreshing. The sheep — content. All was calm and peaceful.

Suddenly, the stillness of the night was shattered. The heavens opened. An angel began to descend. A glorious light broke in upon a darkened world. The shepherds trembled.

The angel said, "Do not be afraid. Behold, I bring you wondrous news! On this day, there shall be joy for every man. A Savior has been born for you. He is Christ the Lord. You will find Him wrapped in swaddling clothes, and lying in a manger."

After the angel had spoken, the Choirs of Heaven raised their voices. "Glory to God in the Highest. Peace on earth to all men."

You and I have heard this story over and over again. It is a beautiful story. But what does it mean? What does it mean, "Unto you, a Savior has been born?"

It means that in Bethlehem, on that silent and holy night of long ago, God took on our flesh and blood and became man. It means God broke into our world to seek our deliverance and salvation, to suffer crucifixion by our hands.

You and I are in no way deserving of what God has done for us. But then, it was not possible for the Loving Father in Heaven to close His Heart to our needs. It was not possible for Him to sit back and watch our helplessness without a Savior. It was not possible for Him to watch His children perish. He, therefore, gave us the Lord Jesus Christ.

Jesus came not to minister unto one nation, but to all nations. He came not to minister unto one class of people, but to all classes. He came to minister unto the miserable and guilty in every land. He came to minister unto your brethren. He came to minster unto you.

Are you weary and in need? Are you burdened with trials and tribulations? Are you lost and full of sin? Are you overcome with hopelessness and fear? Are you despairing and lonely?

"Unto you, a Savior has been born."

My friends, God has come to us in the Person of Jesus Christ. All is well!

The angels were joyful because He came! The shepherds were joyful because He came! If you open your heart and life to Jesus Christ, you too will be joyful.

On this night of nights, the Loving Father in Heaven opens the door to eternal joy and blessings, for those who believe in the One He has sent.

Prayer:

Heavenly Father, You have done great things for us. Unto us this night in the city of David, a Savior has been born which is Christ the Lord. We make a joyful noise unto You. We humbly thank You for Him, Who took upon Himself the form of a servant and was made in the likeness of men to minister unto our every need. Fill us with Your Holy Spirit so His Coming will not be in vain. May the light He brings, destroy the shadows of darkness which hover over us. Bless us with the peace only He can give, especially when we are bending beneath life's crushing load. AMEN.

(For the continuation of this Prayer, see "PRAYER" on page 2 in the Suggestions segment)

Hymn: "Silent Night"

Do You Have Room for Him?

Hymn: "Away in a Manger"

Scripture Lesson: Luke 2: 1-7

Sermon: "Do You Have Room for Him?"

Mary and Joseph, expecting their firstborn child at any moment, arrived in the city of Bethlehem. They went to the Village Inn to secure lodging for the night. The innkeeper informed them, "I'm sorry — I have not room. My inn is full."

Fortunately, Mary and Joseph eventually found a stable where they could spend the night. Before the night was over, Mary had delivered her firstborn child.

What an experience this must have been for Mary. Who explained to the poor girl what to do? She had to be her own midwife. A manger served as a bed for the newborn infant.

When Jesus was born, the heavens opened. Angels descended to proclaim and celebrate His birth. A glorious light overcame the darkness upon the earth. Shepherds made haste from their field to find the Baby Jesus, so they might kneel at His feet. Wise men and Kings, guided by a star, began a long journey to worship this infant.

What the prophets foretold became reality. The Lord God had finally visited His people. This Child would become the Savior and Deliverer of mankind. He would establish a new covenant with God's children. He would give peace and joy to men. He would give hope. He would give life.

Jesus Christ has been born.

On this Christmas, Jesus stands at the door of your heart. He inquires, "Do you have room for Me? I was born that you might know the Way and Truth — that you might have eternal life. I was born to answer your every need. Here I stand. Will you invite Me into your heart?"

Will you, likened unto the inn-keeper, say, "Sorry, no vacancy. My heart is already full of other guests."?

So many of us have filled the spaces within our hearts with the love of worldly things — the hunger for money, the thirst for success, the longing to climb the social ladder, the desire to satisfy self. We have crowded our hearts with endless anxieties.

It is said that the Bethlehem innkeeper remarked later, "I could have filled my lap with silver and gold, if only I had rooms for all the people who came to the door that night. Yet, there was One who came, Whom I would not have turned away for all the silver and gold in the world. If only I had made room for Him. I could have rearranged my guests. But I was a busy man. I was running a business and making money. How was I to know Who He was?"

Let us learn something from this innkeeper. Before it becomes too late, let us do some rearranging within our hearts. It is essential that you find room for Jesus.

My friends, Jesus Christ stands at the door of your heart. He wants to be your Savior. What do you say?

Will you say, "I'm sorry — I have no room. My heart is full of other guests."?

OR will you say, "Enter, Lord! Be my Savior. Give me peace and joy. Give me hope. Give me eternal life!"

Prayer:

Dear Heavenly Father, we humbly thank You for the blessing of Christmas. Unto us a Savior has been born. Help us receive this Savior. Help us now ask:

"OH HOLY CHILD OF BETHLEHEM,

DESCEND TO US WE PRAY;

CAST OUT OUR SIN, AND ENTER IN,

BE BORN IN US TODAY."

We pray You fill us with Your Spirit. Grant us the faith to see the newborn Savior as our counselor when perplexed; our companion when lonely; our comforter when in sorrow; our helper when in need; our health when afflicted; our hope when dying. AMEN.

(For the continuation of this Prayer, see "PRAYER" on page 2 in the Suggestions segment)

<u>Hymn</u>: "O How Shall I Receive Thee"

A Necessary Trip

Hymn: "I Need Thee Every Hour"

Scripture Lesson: Mark 10: 32-34

Sermon: "A Necessary Trip"

During the course of our lives, we have taken many trips. Some have been long; others have been short. Perhaps we have traveled to another state in the union, or even abroad, either for the purpose of business or pleasure. Perhaps we only journeyed to a nearby town or city to visit relatives or friends. Some of our trips have been necessary and some have not. But have we ever taken a trip which has not proven to be beneficial in some respect?

Today is Ash Wednesday, the first day of Lent. During this Lenten Season, we are urged to take a trip which would most certainly be classified as "necessary." This journey will not be a short one. It will take several weeks. It will not be a pleasure cruise, but it should prove to be extremely educational and beneficial. How much will you learn? How meaningful and successful will this venture be? Only you can answer these questions.

In the 18th chapter of the Gospel of Saint Luke, Verses 31-34, Jesus said to His disciples, "Listen to Me. Behold we shall now go to Jerusalem, and everything that has been written by the prophets about the Son of Man will come true. He will be handed over to the unbelievers. They will jeer, insult and spit upon Him. They will flog and kill Him. But, He will rise again on the Third Day." But the disciples did not understand what He said. His words were confusing to them.

It was not unusual for Jesus to tell His disciple they were going to Jerusalem. They had been there before with Jesus to celebrate the Feast of the Passover. But never before had the Master talked about being ill-treated, about suffering and death, and about rising from the dead after three days. Never before had He inferred this would be His last journey to the Holy City. The disciples were unable to understand what Jesus was attempting to tell them. Do we? Are we fully aware of what Christ was saying when He told His disciples, "Behold, we shall go to Jerusalem?"

Here is the WHY of Lent. It is necessary for us during the next several weeks to go to Jerusalem, so that we may better understand the deep significance of the things that are about to come to pass in the life of the Lord Jesus Christ.

On this journey, we shall hear and see children and adults sing songs of praise to Jesus as He enters Jerusalem as King. But, we shall also hear and see an angry mob shout, "Crucify Him." We will see the trusted disciples desert the beloved Master, one by one — the loneliness and agony Jesus endured as He prayed in the Garden of Gethsemane, the unbearable suffering and brutal death Christ encountered at the hands of His enemies, and the love which the Savior showered upon mankind from the Cross. We will see all of this and much more. And then, when His suffering is over, we will see a victory — a victory that will at last bring peace and comfort and joy into our hearts.

So that we might better see and understand, let us day by day during this Holy Journey drink deeply from the spring of prayer and become devout students of the Bible.

And, as we see — we shall be ashamed. For Christ Jesus suffered not for Himself, but for you and me. You and I are responsible for what Christ Jesus had to endure. He suffered and died so that we might have forgiveness for our sins.

My friends, "Behold, He goes up to Jerusalem. Behold, you and I must go up to Jerusalem with Him."

Is this trip necessary? If we do not make this journey with Christ Jesus, we will not truly understand the purpose of His life; the meaning of His Cross; the significance of Easter Sunday Morning.

Prayer:

Lord, help us through these Holy Days of Lent to walk with Jesus during His passion, so we might better comprehend the true reason for His bitter suffering and death. Help us to see how He Who knew no sin endured the shame on the Cross, so that we who believe in Him might not perish because of our sins, but have eternal life. As we contemplate His precious sacrifice necessary for our redemption, help us to lament the evil we have nourished, and by a lively and heartfelt faith obtain deliverance from the wages of our opposition to You. AMEN.

(For the continuation of this Prayer, see "PRAYER" on page 2 in the Suggestions segment)

Hymn: "Just as I Am, Without One Plea"

Father, Forgive Them, for They Know Not What They Do

Hymn: "Love Divine, All Loves Excelling"

Scripture Lesson: Luke 23: 32-34

Sermon: "Father, Forgive Them, for They Know Not What They Do"

The Bible tells us, "Pilate handed Jesus over to the soldiers. When they had finished mocking Him, they led Jesus away. A great crowd was present. When the procession reached Golgotha, which interpreted means 'The Place of the Skull', they crucified Him."

Jesus had been nailed to the Cross. He suffered all the excruciating pain of crucifixion. But He uttered no cry of anguish.

I suppose many expected Jesus to curse those responsible for His miserable plight — expected Him to express some desire for revenge. After all, would this not be the way they would respond if they encountered the same circumstances?

But, instead of hearing words of malice, they heard, "Father, forgive them, for they know not what they do."

These Words from the Cross reveal the love of Christ for all men. This is "Love Divine, All Other Loves Excelling." This is love so extraordinary, it passes all human understanding. As a window is used to look in or out, so can we use the First Word from the Cross as a window to see into the soul of Jesus Christ. There, we behold nothing but beauty.

The Cross of Christ has been called the "Great Intercession." In the First Word from the Cross, Jesus not only intercedes for His contemporaries, but for all mankind. He intercedes for you and for me. Whether we want to admit it or not, we have all played a role in nailing Jesus to the Cross. Remember, our Lord was crucified because of sin.

If we are of the smug opinion that our lives are any cleaner than the lives of the contemporaries of Jesus, we are making a grave mistake. You and I give way to the same evil temptation, the same anxieties, the same worldly impulses. For example, the greed for worldly possessions which caused Judas to betray the Master is the same greed that causes us to lay up treasures on earth, rather than in Heaven.

The fear Peter possessed, and which caused him to deny knowing Christ three times, is the same fear for self which causes us to deny Christ in a non-Christian environment.

The jealousy and envy, the craftiness and hatred which caused Caiaphas and Annas, the Scribes and the Pharisees, to plot against our Lord's Life, are the same elements which have caused mankind to make this world what it is today.

The blindness of Herod, which prevented him from seeing his real need for Jesus, is the same blindness which prevents us from being more conscientious about daily Bible reading and prayer.

The desire to possess worldly security, which prompted Pilate to give Jesus over to His enemies, is the same desire which drives us to obtain worldly security regardless of what it costs others.

There was the mob that shouted, "Crucify Him, crucify Him." There were the soldiers who drove the nails. These personalities did what they were encouraged and told to do. They acted without giving serious thought to what they were doing. Do you always give serious thought to God's Holy Will before you act or speak?

My friends, you and I are sinners. We should be appalled at the evil we support, and the good we leave undone.

But Jesus prays — He implores, "Father, forgive them, for they know not what they do."

<u>Prayer</u>:

Dear God, the Father of us all, we thank You for the love and mercy You have revealed unto us through Jesus. We pray You to fill us with Your Holy Spirit. Make us see that Your Son willingly permitted His precious blood to flow freely, so we might be reconciled unto You. Make us see how our sins made the horror and tragedy of His Cross necessary. Grant that we might follow His example. Help us to love and forgive those who wrong us, as readily as You are willing to love and forgive us. AMEN.

(For the continuation of this Prayer, see "PRAYER" on page 2 in the Suggestions segment)

Hymn: "O Jesus, Thou Art Standing"

Truly, I Say unto You, This Very Day You Will Be With Me in Paradise

Hymn: "There's a Wideness in God's Mercy"

Scripture Lesson: Luke 23: 39-43

Sermon: "Truly, I Say unto You, This Very Day You Will Be With Me in Paradise"

The Holy Scriptures declare, "Two criminals were led out with Jesus for execution. At a place outside the walls of Jerusalem, called the 'Skull', the three were crucified."

It was to one of these criminals, Jesus spoke His Second Word from the Cross: "Truly, I say unto you, this very day you will be with Me in Paradise."

We know very little concerning these criminals. We know even less about the crimes for which they had been convicted. Their relationship to the underworld is a mystery to us.

However, we do know these men had broken the law. They had been caught, convicted, and sentence to death. Now, they hung on a cross — one on the right of Jesus, and the other on His left.

One of these criminals continued in his sin. He joined the others in their jeers and abuse of Jesus. He sarcastically demanded, "Do you not profess to be the Christ? If you are what you claim to be, then why don't you save yourself, and then save us?"

The other criminal admonished his comrade in crime. "Are you not afraid of God, even when you are receiving the same punishment as He? We justly deserve our punishment, but this Man has not committed a wrongful act in His life."

There can be little doubt. This second criminal experienced a change of heart. As he hung nailed to his cross, knowing death would soon take him, he must have trembled with fear at the way he had corrupted and squandered the life God had given him.

He also heard the prayer of Jesus for those who had crucified Him. "Father, forgive them, for they know not what they do." This man, whose philosophy had been "every man for himself," had been incredibly moved by Jesus.

Up to this point, his words had only been directed to his companion. But now, turning to Jesus, he pleaded, "Remember me, when you come into your Kingdom."

The most amazing fact about this request was the faith it revealed in Jesus. The Lord had ignored the remarks of those who had crucified Him. He had ignored the remarks of the other criminal. But He did not ignore the beseeching plea of this man.

Jesus grants a full pardon. "Truly, I say unto you, this very day you will be with Me in Paradise." This criminal had lain upon Christ the weight of his sins; the weight of his soul; the weight of his eternity. And Jesus accepted the burden.

The story of the criminals crucified with Jesus portrays man as he exists today; portrays you and me. As the result of our sin, we are all criminals in the sight of God. You and I have all been convicted and condemned to death.

We have come to a fork in the road. We must make a decision. We can follow one of two paths. We can follow in the footsteps of the first criminal and continue in our sin. OR, we can follow in the footsteps of the second criminal. We can look at the lives which God has given us and see how we are corrupting and squandering them. With the help of the Holy Spirit, we also can experience a change of heart.

Remember, these two criminals had an edge on us. They knew when they would die. They had ample opportunity to make the necessary preparations. One took advantage of this opportunity. The other did not. On the other hand, you and I do not know the day or the hour. Therefore, now is the time to watch and pray. Now is the time to make the necessary preparations.

My friends, if we take advantage of the opportunity Jesus Christ gives us now, then on the day death does beckon us, we can be assured we will be with Him in Paradise.

Prayer:

O Merciful God, we humbly thank You for the precious gift of Your Son, through Whom You have given us the opportunity to be redeemed. For we, like sheep, have gone astray. We have continually turned to our own ways. Our sins are not hidden from You. We are all criminals in Your sight. We ask You, therefore, to fill us with Your Holy Spirit. Guide and direct us. Help us while there is time, as You helped the criminal crucified with Jesus, to accept Him as our Lord and Savior so we might be with Him in Paradise. AMEN.

(For the continuation of this Prayer, see "PRAYER" on page 2 in the Suggestions segment)

Hymn: "I Lay My Sins on Jesus"

Woman, Behold Your Son! Behold, Your Mother!

Hymn: "Christ for the World We Sing"

Scripture Lesson: John 19: 23-27

Sermon: "Woman, Behold Your Son! Behold, Your Mother!"

The Bible tells us, "While the soldiers were drawing lots for His garments, Jesus saw His mother, and a disciple whom He loved standing by her side. He said to His mother, 'Woman, behold your son.' And to the disciple He said, 'Behold your mother.'" Hence Jesus had spoken His Third Word from the Cross.

Being a mother can bring much joy to a woman. It can also bring much sorrow and grief.

How proud Mary must have been to have a Son like Jesus. She could have walked down any Main Street, holding her head high. Her heart must have been a storehouse filled with hopes.

But consider her bitter grief as she stood only a few feet away from the Cross upon which Jesus had been crucified. Helpless, she watched the soldiers drive nails through the flesh of the Son she loved so dearly. She looked at her Son's bruised and bleeding body, but was unable to care for His wounds. Truly, Mary endured as much torment in her heart as did her Son upon His Cross.

At the time of the crucifixion, it is believed that Joseph had passed away, leaving Mary a widow. Now, her Son was dying. Indeed, Jesus was enduring great physical and mental anguish. But in spite of His intense suffering, His eyes penetrated the jeering crowd at the foot of His Cross. They centered upon His widowed mother, and His beloved disciple John. He remembered her deep affection and tender care — her strong and gentle love. He recalled the companionship of John.

Jesus was aware of the tormenting ordeal Mary and John were experiencing. He was aware of the countless needs they would encounter in the future. From His Cross, He said, "Woman, behold your son! Behold your mother." With hands nailed to the Cross, He was unable to point out the two to which He spoke. However, either an accustomed look or a familiar tone in His voice caused Mary and John to fully grasp the meaning of His Words.

We are told that John took care of Mary until her death. What precious memories and sacred hours these two must have shared, as they made their way through the years together. Mary needed the companionship, protection, and comfort of John. Oh the other hand, John, who was also called "a son of thunder," needed the understanding and gentle influence of Mary.

Even during the few tense moments remaining in His earthly life, Jesus portrayed His heartfelt concern for others. Knowing He would soon give up His Spirit, He therefore had to rely upon Mary and John to do what He could not do Himself.

We are all Marys and Johns. We all have needs. You have needs. I have needs. I can help fulfill your needs, the same as you can help fulfill mine. We are the instruments upon which Jesus Christ must depend to continue His ministry. We will either handicap this ministry, or make the love of Christ Jesus become a living reality.

Luther said, "Although addressed only to Mary and John, the Third Word from the Cross must be taken as a general command to all Christians."

My friends, through Jesus Christ, we become one family. Let us therefore, live as one family. As did Mary and John, let us love — let us assist and counsel, comfort and protect one another, whenever the need arises. "Woman, behold your son! Behold your mother!"

<u>Prayer</u>:

Dear Father of us all, through Jesus we have become one family. Fill us with Your Holy Spirit so that we may truly live as Your children. Continually remind us of Your Son's heartfelt concern for others, even while suffering upon His Cross. Help us follow His example despite our cares and burdens, afflictions and pains. Like Mary and John, we all have needs. Grant, therefore, we may always assist and counsel, comfort and protect one another. Use us as Your instruments through which the love of our Savior continues to flow freely to all men. AMEN.

(For the continuation of this Prayer, see "PRAYER" on page 2 in the Suggestions segment)

Hymn: "Blest Be the Tie That Binds"

My God, My God, Why Hast Thou Forsaken Me?

Hymn: "What a Friend We Have in Jesus"

Scripture Lesson: Matthew 27: 45-54

Sermon: "My God, My God, Why Hast Thou Forsaken Me?"

The Holy Scriptures declares, "After Jesus had been crucified, darkness spread over the whole countryside from noon until three o'clock."

It could be said that this prevailing darkness symbolized the earthly life of Jesus. His life in the flesh was continually being led through the valley of darkness. Within the past twenty-four hours of this life, He had seen His disciples flee in fear. He had been betrayed and denied, ridiculed and tortured by His own people. He had been rejected and forsaken — crucified like a common criminal by those He loved.

For nearly three hours, He had been subjected to all the excruciating pain of crucifixion. His body ached. His strength was rapidly subsiding. Yet, His physical and mental torment lingered on. How much more could He endure?

Under these circumstances, does it surprise us to hear Jesus cry out His Fourth Word from the Cross: "My God, My God, why hast Thou forsaken Me?"

Have we not also encountered darkness? Have we not felt the black clouds surrounding our lives crushing us? Who has not experienced the crippling effects of anxiety — what it means to be alone and forsaken? Have we not wondered if God has abandoned us?

But when darkness does invade our lives, do we follow the example of Jesus Christ?

I personally cannot believe His cry from the Cross was one of despair. This was a cry of faith. This was a prayer to His Father in Heaven.

Perhaps it is true, for an instant, Jesus was not able to feel God's comforting presence. Perhaps for a moment, Jesus struggled with Satan, who was constantly tempting Him. Whatever the case, the cry of Jesus was not, "God, why hast Thou forsaken Me?" but, "MY God, why hast Thou forsaken Me?" The Fourth Word from the Cross was prayed in profound earnestness. The words "MY God, MY God" give evidence of Jesus praying from the depth of His soul to a Father He knew would answer His prayer.

And shortly after His prayer, the suffering of Jesus came to an end. The veil in the Temple was ripped from top to bottom. The rocks on earth were torn asunder. Graves were opened. Even Rome paid homage to Christ by way of Pilate's deputy, who said, "Truly, this was the Son of God." And then, on Easter morning, Jesus Christ rose from the dead! By so doing, He had conquered not only the devil and sin, but death and the grave as well.

Did God forsake Jesus? Surely, the events we have mentioned reveal that He did not!

My friends, the fourth Word from the Cross enables us to better understand that Jesus was truly man. He endured all the physical and mental torture we endure.

But let us not forget, Jesus Christ was also truly God. That is to say, God through Jesus Christ has experienced what it means to be a human being.

Therefore, when darkness grips our human lives, when anguish and affliction torment us, let us never doubt the nearness and mercy of God. Although we may not always feel His presence in time of need, we can be assured He is standing by, ready to deliver us, according to His Holy Will.

<u>Prayer</u>:

MY God, MY God, during our trials and tribulations, grant us Your Holy Spirit. Grant us the faith of Jesus Christ. And, through Him, grant us the light of Easter to replace the darkness of our Good Fridays. AMEN.

(For the continuation of this Prayer, see "PRAYER" on page 2 in the Suggestions segment)

<u>Hymn</u>: "A Mighty Fortress Is Our God"

I Thirst

Hymn: "Rise Up, O Men of God"

Scripture Lesson: John 19: 28-29

Sermon: "I Thirst"

The Bible tells us, "After Jesus was crucified, and knowing all was now finished, He said, 'I thirst'."

"I thirst" was the Fifth Word from the Cross, an expression of true humanity. Thirst — the foremost biological drive of man.

At the time of His crucifixion, Jesus had been offered sour wine, but refused it. We are told that a guild of benevolent women in Jerusalem always prepared a drugged wine for those poor souls condemned to crucifixion. Its purpose was to help kill the pain.

It was this drugged wine which Jesus refused at the time He was being nailed to His Cross.

Jesus must have craved liquid refreshment. No beverage had touched His lips since the night before, when He and His disciples had assembled in the Upper Room.

Since the Upper Room, Jesus had been arrested, tried, and condemned — hauled back and forth through the streets of Jerusalem — bound, tortured, and pushed up the slopes of Calvary. He had been hanging on His Cross for nearly three hours. The air was heavy and humid.

Indeed, the lips of Jesus were parched. His tongue was swollen. Is it any wonder His exhausted physical frame cried out for refreshment? Jesus, knowing all was now finished, said, "I thirst."

The bowl of sour wine was still standing nearby. Upon hearing the Fifth Word, someone soaked a sponge in the wine, placed the sponge upon a spear, and raised it to the lips of Jesus. This someone might have been one of the soldiers. Or, this someone might have been one of the small company of loved ones standing near the cross.

In any case, the person who satisfied the thirst of Jesus was granted a privilege which we cannot but envy. One is reminded of the Words of Jesus, as recorded in the 25th chapter of the Gospel of Saint Matthew. "Come, you have won My Father's Blessing. Take your inheritance which shall be the Kingdom of God. For I was thirsty, and you gave Me Drink."

But you and I need not envy. For we, too, are granted the opportunity to satisfy the thirst of Jesus. Jesus continues to thirst through others. And "inasmuch as you relieve the thirst of my needy brethren, you relieve My thirst. What you do for them, you do for Me, sayeth the Lord."

The thirst which Jesus experienced upon the Cross extended far beyond the physical realm. In order for Him to fulfill His mission of taking away the sin of the world, Jesus had to thirst. To become the fountain of eternal life, Jesus had to pass through a dry and thirsty land. Jesus thirsted, so the door to God's Kingdom would be opened to all men.

Jesus Christ thirsted for your salvation. You can satisfy His thirst by living a life of sacrifice and obedience, devotion and love.

My friends, Christ Jesus has a burning thirst.

He thirsts for the needs of others. Will you not raise the sponge to His lips by providing for the needs of the least of His brethren?

He thirsts for your salvation. Will you not raise the sponge to His lips by giving Him your heart and prayers, life and soul?

Jesus says, "I thirst."

<u>Prayer</u>:

O Lord God, Who gave us Your Precious Son Jesus, we humbly pray that the thirst He endured upon His Cross may not be in vain. We beseech You to fill our hearts with Your Holy Spirit, and enable us to see that His suffering and death were for us. Grant that we may respond to His love.

Grant we may be likened unto the one who raised the sponge to His lips. Help us satisfy His burning thirst for all humanity by ministering unto their temporal and spiritual needs. By Your Grace, enable us to give Him our love and devotion, lives and souls. AMEN.

(For the continuation of this Prayer, see "PRAYER" on page 2 in the Suggestions segment)

Hymn: "Savior, Thy Dying Love"

Who Is This Man Called Jesus?

Hymn: "All Glory, Laud, and Honor"

Scripture Lesson: Matthew 21: 1-10

Sermon: "Who Is This Man Called Jesus?"

Some two thousand, six hundred years ago, a prophet of Israel called Zechariah said to oppressed and afflicted people, "My people, rejoice and shout. For behold, the Lord God will send you a King who shall make His appearance riding upon a donkey, or upon a colt, the foal of donkey. He will be humble and just. He will be triumphant and victorious. He will be your salvation. He will remove the instruments of war and reign by peaceful means. He will rule the world from sea to sea. Through this King, the Lord God will make a covenant with you sealed in blood. Therefore my people, do not despair, for the Lord God will bestow great and wondrous blessings upon you."

The people of Israel waited patiently for their deliverance. The years came and the years slowly passed by, but the prophecy of Zechariah was not fulfilled.

Then, six hundred years after Zechariah had uttered his prophecy, a certain man answering the prophet's description entered Jerusalem at the time of the Passover. His Name was Jesus. Although this Jesus had entered the Holy City on several previous occasions, never before had He appeared riding upon the back of a donkey.

Someone, sensing this might be the fulfillment of Zechariah's prophecy, shouted, "Blessed be the King who comes in the Name of the Lord." The hearts of those assembled were moved, prompting others to also extend warm greetings to this Jesus. Within a few brief moments, Jesus was being given a rousing hero's welcome — a welcome fit for a king. As the procession continued, it became larger and larger. The noise and shouting became louder and louder. Some of the multitude spread palm branches; some spread their garments in the path of Jesus, while others shouted "Hosanna," meaning, "Lord, save us now."

The procession ended. Somewhat disappointed and disillusioned, the crowd slowly melted away. The people began to inquire among themselves, "Who is this man called Jesus?" Is He the One of whom Zechariah spoke, or is He not?

Inasmuch as nothing spectacular had taken place, the people became confused. They had anticipated the Promised Messiah establishing His Kingdom. They had expected Jesus to leap to the pinnacle of the temple — to sunder the clouds of heaven — to summon a vast army of angels and archangels — to eject the Romans from power — and to compel the enemy to bow before Him.

But everything remained calm and peaceful. Much to the people's disappointment, there was no sound of trumpet; no clash of arms; no great military display.

The Palm Sunday crowd of long ago became confused, simply because Jesus did not establish His Kingdom in the manner and by the methods, they thought He would. This is why they inquired among themselves, "Who is this man called Jesus?"

I cannot help but wonder about the many individuals making up today's Palm Sunday crowd. Are any of you confused about this Man called Jesus?

If you can, point to a single man who can master the trials and heartaches, temptations and woes of this life. Only Jesus Christ can say, "Be of good cheer, I have overcome the world." Only He can say, "Come unto Me, all you that labor and are heavy laden, and I will give you rest."

Point to a single man who can do anything about sin. Only Jesus Christ can say, "I am the Good Shepherd Who giveth His life for the sheep who have gone astray." Only He can say, "My blood cleanseth you from all sin."

Point to a single man who can do anything about death. Only Jesus Christ can say, "I am the resurrection and the life. He that believeth in Me, though he were dead, yet shall he live. And whosoever liveth and believeth in Me shall never die." Only Jesus can say, "I am the living bread which came down from Heaven. If any man eats of this bread, he shall live for all eternity."

We can be assured that although the first Palm Sunday crowd may have been wrong in their conclusions regarding how Jesus would establish His Kingdom, they were correct in assuming the prophecy of Zechariah was being fulfilled. Although they may have doubted their actions afterward, they had been right in spreading their garments and palms before Jesus. They had been correct in shouting their "Hosannas." They were speaking the truth by saying that Jesus had come in the Name of the Lord. For Jesus Christ had entered the Holy City in the Name of the Lord God. He had come into our world in the name of the Father in Heaven to save and deliver mankind.

My friends, on that Palm Sunday of long ago, Jesus Christ rode into Jerusalem to establish the Kingdom of God. He was intent upon establishing this Kingdom according to the Heavenly Father's Will, and not in accordance with man's will. And within days, the Kingdom had been established. Jesus had freed the believers from slavery to the powers of the devil and sin, and from death and the grave, so that all who profess Him as Lord and Savior might dwell in His Kingdom forever.

Can there really be any doubts in your mind concerning this Man called Jesus? Truly, He is the One of which the prophet Zechariah spoke.

Therefore, on this Palm Sunday, let us sing loud "Hosannas."

Let us pray from the depths of our souls: "Lord, save us now." Let us shout with stout and believing hearts, "Blessed be this Jesus Christ, who comes in the Name of the Lord God."

<u>Prayer</u>:

Almighty God, our Father and Creator, Who promised by Your prophets to deliver us from our enemies, enable us by Your Holy Spirit to see that Jesus Christ, the One Who rode in triumph into Jerusalem long ago, came in Your Name so we might, through Him, be victorious in all things. We praise You that He came, not as a conqueror to destroy, but as a Messiah to save. We thank You that He came not to create an earthly kingdom, but one in which we can dwell for all eternity. Help us always to accept Him as our King, and permit Him to rule our hearts and minds, lives and souls, so that we may always live in the Kingdom He entered the Holy City to establish. AMEN.

(For the continuation of this Prayer, see "PRAYER" on page 2 in the Suggestions segment)

Hymn: "Ride on, Ride on in Majesty"

It is Finished

Hymn: "In the Cross of Christ I Glory"

Scripture Lesson: Matthew 26: 26-28

Sermon: "It is Finished"

The Holy Scriptures declare, "After Jesus tasted the sponge soaked in sour wine, He cried aloud; 'It is finished.' Then His head fell forward."

The sixth Word from the Cross. "It is finished."

These were the words of a young man who had not reached the prime of life. A man in His early thirties, who had been rejected by those He had come to save. And as a result of this rejection, the list of injustices and torments Jesus endured was a long one.

Now it was over. The end to His humiliation had come.

But this Sixth Word from the Cross was not a cry of human relief. It was the shout of victory. It was the proclamation of a conqueror.

"It is finished." What began in a stable on a silent and holy night had ended. The ministry which the Father in Heaven had sent His only begotten Son to perform had been achieved. The revelation of God to man in the Person of Christ had been completed. The messianic prophecies had been fulfilled. Reconciliation between God and man had been established.

"It is finished." Jesus had come to give His life as a ransom for many. He came as the "Lamb of God that would take away the sins of the world." To free us from our bondage, so we might have life and immortality, a price was demanded. Jesus paid our ransom with His Body and Blood. He willingly drank the bitter content of the cup overflowing, without iniquities — the cup filled with the Wrath of God against our opposition to Him. Now this cup was empty.

"It is finished." The Highway of our redemption has been completed. The road leading to our salvation has been opened to traffic. Now, all anyone has to do is begin his or her journey through Christ Jesus.

My friends, "It is finished."

On this Holy Thursday, because it is finished, the Words of Jesus take on intimate significance for all who come to Him with believing and repentant hearts.

"My Body given for you — My Blood shed for you and for many, for the remission of sins."

Prayer:

Lord God, *it is finished*. We humbly thank You. You are good and Your mercy endures forever. You have established a New Covenant with us. You did so love us, You gave your only begotten Son, that whosoever believeth in Him might not perish, but have everlasting life. We beseech You to fill our hearts and minds with Your Holy Spirit. Do not allow the sufferings and death of Jesus Christ to be in vain. Grant us Your grace to believe He has redeemed us, not with silver and gold, but with His own precious blood. Grant that we always remember, He was wounded for our transgressions and bruised for our iniquities. Give us a victorious faith in Him. Help us travel the Highway, which enables us to partake of those unspeakable joys You have prepared for all who love and follow Him.

(For the continuation of this Prayer, see "PRAYER" on page 2 in the Suggestions segment)

Hymn: "Beneath the Cross of Jesus"

Father, Into Your Hands I Commend My Spirit

Hymn: "Were You There When They Crucified My Lord?"

Scripture Lesson: Luke 23: 44-46

Sermon: "Father, Into Your Hands I Commend My Spirit"

The Bible tells us: "With His last breath, Jesus said; 'Father, into Your hands, I commend My spirit'."

After His Seventh Word from the Cross, Jesus died. He died on that Good Friday long ago.

It is difficult to number the individuals who have expressed confusion concerning the name "Good Friday." Surely, a name such as "Bad Friday" would be much more appropriate.

That particular Friday impresses the majority of us as being the blackest day in human history. Men acting like vicious animals had done their worst. They had committed the most devilish act in all creation. They had killed the Prince of Glory! Defying the Almighty God, they nailed His only begotten Son to a cross!

The Pharisees and Scribes; Judas, Herod, and Pilate; the soldiers, the mob, all played a role in this crucifixion. They were all guilty. But as guilty as they were, this terrible deed was not theirs alone.

The first line of a well-known spiritual confronts us with a question. "Were you there when they crucified my Lord?" We were there! You were there! I was there! Be assured, we played our role in crucifying Jesus by way of our sins.

Actually, whether this day should be considered "Bad Friday" or "Good Friday" depends entirely upon you.

If you only see this day as a time in history when a 180-pound Jewish man, a good and kind man called Jesus, died a horrible death upon a cross and nothing more — then this day is "Bad Friday."

On the other hand, if you believe Jesus Christ is the son of God — if you recognize your role in His crucifixion, and are led to a reformation of heart and life — if you see this day as the time in history when God's Divine Plan for our redemption was reaching its climax — then this day indeed becomes "Good Friday."

GOOD FRIDAY! The day Jesus completed his Father's business. His mission fulfilled; His work finished; His battle over! Jesus had conquered the devil and sin! He was now in the process of conquering death and the grave.

With His last breath, Jesus said, "Father, into Your hands, I commend My spirit." And with these words, He died in perfect peace. The seventh Word from the Cross was a prayer of complete faith. Jesus knew all was well. Without hesitation, He committed His spirit into the Hands of His Heavenly Father, knowing it would be received with love and tenderness.

But let us remember, the absolute faith that Jesus revealed at the end was by no means a last-minute impulse. It was the climax of daily companionship with His Father. All His earthly life, hour by hour and day by day, Jesus had placed Himself in His Father's hands. As the result of this relationship, when the end came, Jesus knew He was making a deposit in a safe and secure place.

My friends, if you believe, then this is truly "Good Friday" then be assured when you walk through the valley of the shadow of death, you need fear no evil.

Jesus Christ has gone before us. And where he has gone, He has prepared the Way. We can follow Him in confidence. He has not only taught us how to live, but also how to die.

If we, through Him, place ourselves in the hands of God, with our last breath we can also say, with absolute faith, "Father, into Your hands, I commend my spirit."

Prayer:

Heavenly Father, help us always remember with thankful hearts what You have done for us through Your only begotten Son. He bore for us the suffering and death of the Cross, so we might be Your children and be strengthened by Your grace. Fill us with Your Holy Spirit. Grant that we see Jesus Christ as our only hope of salvation. Give us the necessary faith in Him, so that through His victory, we might overcome the enemies of this world. Whatever the adversary, whether it be the torment of sin or the burden of affliction or the fear of death, enable us through Him to daily commend our spirits into your Hands, knowing they will be received with love and mercy. AMEN.

(For the continuation of this Prayer, see "PRAYER" on page 2 in the Suggestions segment)

Hymn: "Pass Me Not, O Gentle Savior"

The Miracle of Miracles

Hymn: "The Strife Is Over, the Battle Done"

Scripture Lesson: John 11: 21-27

Sermon: "The Miracle of Miracles"

Easter, the "Miracle of Miracles." Easter, the most spectacular event in the history of man.

"Jesus Christ has risen from the dead. His tomb is empty."

Indeed, the Resurrection of Christ Jesus is a historical fact. The evidence of this event is so striking, it doesn't seem possible anyone could resist it.

Let us look at some of this evidence; the testimony given by those closest to Jesus.

There can be little doubt that the Resurrection of Jesus Christ was not expected, not even by His few devoted followers. Neither the Holy Scriptures, nor Jesus Himself, had led His disciples to the conviction that He would rise from the dead. The manner in which His followers acted at the time of the crucifixion verify this fact. Before the crucifixion, they had proven themselves cowards. After the crucifixion, they were plunged into profound despair.

Then came that Easter morning. The women, who wanted to anoint His body, were amazed to find the huge stone in front of His tomb rolled away. They were even more amazed to find the tomb empty. They were astounded to hear, "Jesus Christ has Risen." They made great haste to inform the others. The others did not believe. They had to investigate for themselves.

Now, the amazement which the women expressed and the disbelief the others conveyed, indicates that the followers of Jesus had not taken His body. We can be certain that the enemies of Jesus had not taken His body, for this would have promoted the thought among the people that Jesus was truly the Promised Messiah. And we can be assured that thieves had not taken His body, because of the Roman guards surrounding the tomb.

Therefore, the only explanation for the empty tomb was that Jesus Christ had risen from the dead. This is further established when Jesus appeared to His disciples, as well as others. His appearance to the disciples is substantiated by the transformation that took place in their lives. They were no longer fearful; no longer cowards or slow to believe. They possessed a brand-new faith. Even though they were sheep in the midst of wolves, they preached the Gospel with determination and zeal, in spite of the constant threat of persecution.

Certainly, something happened in the lives of these followers to transform them so completely. Nothing can explain this change, except the power of the Resurrection.

Many noted scholars of history have stated that no historical fact is more substantially proven by collective evidence than the Resurrection of Jesus Christ.

The question is: *"What does this Miracle of Miracles mean for you and me?"*

The Resurrection of Jesus Christ means He is alive forever more. He lives to answer your prayers and forgive your sins. He lives to heal and calm, comfort and guide. He lives to abide in every heart and every home that would receive Him. He lives to bestow hope and peace upon all who would have these blessings.

The Resurrection of Jesus Christ means He has conquered the devil and sin, death and the grave. It means if we abide in Him and He in us, we shall share His victory. It means death, for the believer, is only a passageway of brief darkness which leads to the Golden City of Eternal Life. It means GLORY – not doom.

The Resurrection means, as the blazing sun transforms the night of darkness and storm; the Living Jesus can transform your life, as He did the lives of the disciple long ago.

Truly, blessed are you, though you have not seen, and yet believe!

My friends, hear the words of the Resurrected Christ!

"I am He that liveth and was dead. Behold! I have the Keys of Hell and Death!"

"He that believeth in Me, though he were dead, yet shall he live. And, whosoever liveth and believeth in Me shall never die!"

"I am the door. By Me, if any man enters in, he shall be saved!"

Prayer:

Almighty God, we humbly thank You for the triumphant victory Your Son Jesus Christ has won over death and the grave. We thank You for the new and glorious life He has obtained for all who believe in Him. Through Him, You have opened the Gates of Heaven. We implore You; send us Your Holy Spirit. Although we have not seen, help us to believe. Grant us Your grace so when doubts assault us, we will not waver. Help us, through Him, to overcome all that separates us from You.

Enable all He has done for us to become the bright dawn of a new day which supplants our dark, stormy nights. Make us partakers of the eternal blessings He has prepared for all who love and follow Him. AMEN.

(For the continuation of this Prayer, see "PRAYER" on page 2 in the Suggestions segment)

Hymn: "O for a Thousand Tongues to Sing"

Keep the Light Blazing

Hymn: "Come, Gracious Spirit, Heavenly Dove"

Scripture Lesson: John: 14: 25-31, Acts 2: 1-11

Sermon: "Keep the Light Blazing"

A man lost his way in a dark cave. The light of the candle he carried lit the perilous path he walked.

Markings upon the walls of the cave indicated the direction he should go. The light he carried enabled him to see these markings. The light helped him safely pass the treacherous tunnels that could lead him astray; the deep pits into which he could fall. The light was his hope.

How cautiously he carried the candle. How carefully he shielded the light from a sudden gust of wind; from droplets of water; from anything that might extinguish it.

Our lives are to be likened unto this man, making his way through the dark cave. Human nature makes our path not only dark, but dangerous.

If the Lord God gave us no light, we could never find our way to Holiness and Heaven. We could never reach our Father's Home. We would perish in the darkness.

Pentecost, the third major festival in the church year; on this day we commemorate the coming of the Holy Spirit, the birth of the Holy Christian Church.

When Jesus spoke of His ascension, His followers expressed concern as to what would happen to them without His leadership and counsel. He informed them that His departure would not mean they would be without Divine presence. He would send them the counselor, the Holy Spirit.

The Holy Spirit would bear witness to God the Father and God the Son. He would call and gather. He would enlighten men concerning the teachings of God given by Jesus. He would enlighten men in the Ways of Truth and Righteousness. He would be the light from Heaven that guides and directs men along life's road. Without the Holy Spirit, men would live in utter darkness.

The followers of Jesus would not be left by themselves. On the Day of Pentecost, the Savior's Promise was fulfilled. The presence of the Holy Spirit, as indicated in the 2nd chapter of Acts, verses 1-11, was witnessed in the lives of countless men and women. Today, His presence is being experienced in the lives of untold individuals.

A question frequently asked is: "How do I know; how can I be sure the Holy Spirit is present within my life?"

A small boy was flying a balloon filled with gas on a very windy day. The balloon soared high into the sky; so high, it climbed above the low passing clouds. Observing the boy looking upward, a man standing nearby inquired, "What are you looking at?"

The boy replied, "I am looking for my balloon."

"Your balloon?" the man asked. "I do not see any balloon."

"I know," said the lad, "but I sure can feel it pulling."

So it is with the Holy Spirit. Although we are unable to see Him, we can feel His presence.

Whenever we become aware of our need for the Holy Christian Church, we can be assured that God's Spirit is present within our hearts. The Church is the Workshop of the Holy Spirit through which, in a special way, He calls and gathers and enlightens; through which He bears witness to the Father and Son by way of the Word and Sacraments.

We can be assured of the Holy Spirit's presence whenever we find comfort in our prayers and Bible in time of anxiety or affliction — whenever a truth of a sermon or hymn makes an impact upon our lives — whenever a breathless view of nature directs our attention to the Creator — whenever we find the right guidance in times of trouble or danger — whenever we become bearers of the necessary light in times of darkness.

We can be assured of the Holy Spirit's presence whenever we are strengthened in our God-man relationship.

My friends, when God created the earth, He said, "Let there be light," and there was light. Something very similar happens to the man who allows the Holy Spirit to enter his heart.

Without the Holy Spirit, man blindly stumbles about in the darkness of this world.

However, when the Holy Spirit enters his heart, there is light. There is guidance and direction. Life has meaning. It becomes a holy venture.

If you do not feel the nearness of God, whatever the circumstances you encounter, you are allowing worldly interference to extinguish the light of the Holy Spirit.

<u>Prayer</u>:

Heavenly Father, we thank You for Your Holy Spirit. We thank You for the light and guidance, inspirations and comfort which come from Him. We pray He may ever direct us unto You and Your Son. Send Him into our hearts, that we might have light to overcome the darkness of life's road. Grant He may so rule our hearts, that He may teach us all things and lead us into all Truth; that He may enlighten and sanctify. Grant that He may strengthen our faith in Christ Jesus, through Whom all things are possible. Grant we may always feel the nearness of Your loving presence, and know You are our rock and fortress, refuge and strength. AMEN.

(For the continuation of this Prayer, see "PRAYER" on page 2 in the Suggestions segment)

<u>Hymn</u>: "Creator Spirit, by Whose Aid"

What Do We Believe About God?

Hymn: "Come Thou Almighty King"

Scripture Lesson: John 16:12-15

Sermon: What Do We Believe About God?

So many have asked the question, "What do we believe about God?" Simply put, our belief is stated in the Doctrine of the Holy Trinity.

This Doctrine is summarized in any one of the three Creeds which the Church confesses; namely, The Apostles' Creed, The Nicene Creed, and The Athanasian Creed. Although you may be unfamiliar with The Athanasian Creed, which is rarely used because of its length, you are certainly familiar with The Apostles' and Nicene creeds. These three Creeds are statements of our Christian Faith – they are statements concerning what we believe about God.

We believe God reveals and expresses Himself unto us in three different Persons. Yet, He always remains One God. He reveals and expresses Himself unto us as God the Father – as God the Son – as God the Holy Spirit.

We believe God the Father is our Creator and Sustainer. We believe God the Son is our Redeemer. We believe God the Holy Spirit is our Sanctifier – the One Who makes us holy.

As the Father, we know God as the One Who gave us life – as the One Who daily sustains the physical, mental, and spiritual needs of this life.

As the Son Jesus Christ, we know God as the One Who shows us the Way and the Truth — as the One Who frees us from our slavery to sin, the devil, death, and the grave.

As the Holy Spirit, we know God as the One Who sanctifies and make us holy – as the One Who enables sinners to become saints – as the One Who gives us strength and guidance in all spiritual matters. We know Him as the One Who directs us to Jesus Christ.

As stated by Luther, in his explanation regarding the third article of The Apostles' Creed: "I believe that I cannot by my own reason or strength believe in Jesus Christ. Nor can I on my own come to Him. It is the Holy Spirit Who calls me through the Gospel, enlightens me with His Gifts, sanctifies and preserves me in the true faith."

Hence, the Doctrine of the Holy Trinity is simply the teaching of the Christian Church, which professes that even though God remains One God, He reveals and expresses Himself unto us in three different Persons.

Consider if you will, how I as an individual am a father, son, and pastor. I remain the same individual but reveal and express myself in three different ways. Also consider that H2O is the formula for water, ice, and snow. The same substance reveals and expresses itself in three different ways. So with God. He remains One God – One substance, giving humanity three expressions of His Being.

Our human reasoning may make it difficult for us to fully grasp the Doctrine of the Holy Trinity. But remember the words of Saint Paul: "I stand amazed at the complexity of God's Wisdom and Knowledge. How can any man ever hope to fully understand His reasons for action or fully explain His methods of working? For what man has known the Mind of God? What man has been His counselor? For from God, through God, to God are all things."

My friends, may the blessing of the Almighty God the Father, the Son, and the Holy Spirit be with you always.

<u>Prayer</u>:

Almighty God, we humbly thank You for the revelation of Your Being. You reveal Yourself unto us in three Persons – as the Father, as the Son Jesus, and as the Holy Spirit — yet You remain One.

We know You as the One who gave us life – as the One Who daily sustains the physical, mental, and spiritual needs of this life. We thank You for these blessings.

We know You as the One Who shows us The Way and Truth – as the One Who frees us from our slavery to sin and the devil, death, and the grave. We thank You for these blessings.

We know You as the One Who sanctifies and makes us holy – as the One Who enables sinners to become saints – as the One Who gives us knowledge and guidance and strength in all spiritual matters. We thank You for these blessings.

May the Blessings of God the Father, the Son Jesus, and the Holy Spirit be with us always. AMEN.

(For the continuation of this Prayer, see "PRAYER" on page 2 in the Suggestions segment)

Hymn: "O Trinity of Blessed Light"

It Is so Easy to Forget

Hymn: "We Gather Together to Ask the Lord's Blessings"

Scripture Lesson: Luke 17: 11-19

Sermon: "It Is so Easy to Forget"

Before the Pilgrims left the "old world" for the "new," the Rev. John Robinson read to them the words recorded in the 12th chapter of Genesis, verse 2.

"And the Lord God said; 'I will make you into a great nation. I will bless you, and make your name great. And you shall become a blessing.'"

There is a remarkable resemblance between God's chosen children of Israel, and we Americans — between the land of "milk and honey" which God promised to the Israelites, and America.

Our text for this Thanksgiving is the 8th chapter of Deuteronomy, verses 7-20.

"For the Lord your God shall bring you into a good and wondrous land. This land shall be a land of brooks and fountains and springs, flowing forth in valleys and mountains. It shall be a land of wheat and barley — a land of fruitful trees and vines. It shall be a land whose stones are iron, and out of whose hills you can dig copper. It shall indeed be a land of milk and honey — a land in which you can eat bread without scarcity — a land in which you will lack nothing. And you shall eat and be full."

This describes the land that the Lord God promised to the children of Israel. But is it not also a vivid portrayal of the land in which you and I now live? America — a land of beauty and abundance, prosperity and freedom. Truly, the Lord God has richly blessed us.

But, let us continue with our text. The author gives a stern warning to the Israelites.

"Take heed, lest you forget the Lord your God when you have eaten and are full — when you have built houses and enjoy the comforts of them —

when your herds and flocks, silver and gold have multiplied. Take heed, lest you forget it was the Lord your God who brought you out of the land of Egypt where you were held in bondage. It was the Lord God who led you through the terrible wilderness, the wilderness with the fiery serpents and scorpions and the dry and thirsty ground. It was the Lord God who brought you water out of the rock, and who fed you in the wilderness."

In the midst of plenty, it was so easy for the children of Israel to forget it was the Lord God Who provided, sustained, and guided them during their hardships and trials. In the midst of abundance, it was so easy to forget it was the Lord God Who had lavished His Gifts upon them.

"Take heed, lest you forget." This was the warning given to the Israelites. The same warning applies to us.

How very difficult it is, as we sit in our homes surrounded by all the comforts we enjoy, to give serious thought to what has transpired in this land to make America what it is today.

For example, we give little thought to the early settlers who fought the dangers and weather, as well as the pains of starvations and illness, in order to develop this land. We give little thought to the great wars in which this country has been engaged to preserve freedom.

As a nation, we too have certainly experienced periods of hardship and trial. But do you not believe the Lord God has provided, sustained, and guided? Do you not believe He has lavishly showered His gifts upon us?

Indeed, it is so easy to forget.

"Take heed." Failure to heed this warning will surely cause us to encounter great difficulties, as a people and a nation. The danger confronting us is well expressed in our text.

"If you do not take heed, you will think in your hearts that your own powers and the might of your hands have gotten you this wealth and these comforts. You must remember the Lord your God, for it is He and He alone who has supplied you with the means to obtain what you have. If you do forget the Lord God, you will begin to worship and serve other gods. If this happens, I solemnly warn you on this day that you shall perish. Like the nations that perished before you, so shall you also perish."

The danger which confronts us is that prosperity leads to forgetfulness. When in need, we look to God. But when all is well, we have the tendency to forget Him. This is human nature. Prosperity can turn the eyes of man from the Lord God toward self. Prosperity can lead man to self-glorification.

What is prosperity doing to us as a people and a nation?

I wonder, as I consider the egocentric and materialistic outlook that we share concerning life. I wonder, as I observe the attitude of countless individuals. I wonder, as I read the daily headlines.

Do you not agree there is need for concern? In this 21st century, far too many human beings have become children of prosperity. Far too few remain children of God.

"Take heed, lest you forget." Thanksgiving must be more than a day in which we stuff ourselves with turkey and sweet potatoes. It must be more than a mere holiday in which we watch parades and football games. It must be a day of remembrance. It must be a day in which we remember what the Lord our God has done for us.

Remembrance will strengthen our faith, will make us humble and teach us to rely more upon our Creator. Remembrance of what the Lord God has done for you and me will nourish a feeling of gratitude and promote a heartfelt desire to obey His Will. Remembrance will make every day a "day of thanksgiving."

Who is responsible for this great land which gives bread without scarcity and enables her people to live life so fully? The answer is the Lord God! He and He alone is responsible. It is He Who has made and blessed us, and not we ourselves. You and I are only His people — the sheep of His pasture.

My friends, "take heed, lest you forget." You have eaten and are full. Now, for your own welfare, call to remembrance the love and goodness and mercy of the Lord God, and raise your voices. Be thankful unto Him, and bless His Name.

Prayer:

O Lord God, You are the Creator of Heaven and Earth, the sustainer of all life, the source of all power, and the giver of all good gifts. We, as the sheep of Your pasture, humbly praise Your Holy Name. We thank You for this land of plenty and abundance, for the sun and rain, moon and stars. We thank You for the roof over our heads and the food on our tables, the clothing on our bodies, and our senses, which enable us to enjoy the wonders of Your world. We thank You for our loved ones; for those who care and minister unto us. We thank You for all we take for granted, both people and things. Lord, we thank You not only for our daily bread, but also the Bread of Life which You so abundantly give us through Christ Jesus. Fill us with Your Holy Spirit, and enable us always to call to remembrance Your countless benefits, and to count our endless blessings. Continue to open Your hand and satisfy our needs, whatever they may be. AMEN.

(For the continuation of this Prayer, see "PRAYER" on page 2 in the Suggestions segment)

Hymn: "Come, Ye Thankful People, Come"

A General Prayer

Almighty and Merciful God, our Creator and gracious provider, the author and giver of all good and perfect things, we humbly bow our heads before You with the certainty You are our Shepherd and Loving Father in Heaven. We are the sheep of Your pasture. We are Your children.

It is because we are Your children that we now come to You in prayer.

As You know, due to our living in this world of imperfection, we encounter endless afflictions and burdens, concerns and doubts. We therefore implore You to help us. Help us to rise above the torment created by worldly anxieties — above the valleys of despair. Help us to cast our cares, whatever they may be, upon You; knowing that You care for us — that You will not forsake us during times of special need.

Heavenly Father, fill our anxious hearts with Your Holy Spirit so we might be better aware of Your loving presence. Give us light to overcome our darkness. Give us the assurance that You are watching over us and that all is well. Strengthen us spiritually, mentally, and physically.

Merciful Father, we give You our heartfelt praise and gratitude for the gift of Your Son, Jesus. Not only has He made it possible for us to receive forgiveness for our sins, but He has also shown us the Way and the Truth. Through Him, we can experience hope, relief and peace — we can taste victory. For He has conquered all our earthly enemies, including death.

Compassionate Father, we petition You for mercy. We beg You for the sake of Jesus to forgive our sins against You and our fellow men. Help us to overcome our weaknesses. Guide and direct us in such a way that we may always follow in our Master's footsteps — follow His example. Help us to forever remember that while Jesus dwelt among us in the flesh, He also encountered pain and agony, affliction and conflict and torment. Yet, He always committed Himself into Your loving hands, and You always provided Him with the nourishment He required to surmount.

Loving Father, we ask You to abundantly bless and comfort, sustain and uplift anyone in this vast world of ours who hungers and thirst for Your mercy and grace. Bless our loved ones, wherever they may be at this moment, who we name in our hearts before You. Bless those who in any way minister unto us — the doctors, nurses, rescue workers, and all others.

Heavenly Father, help us remember the Words of Jesus: "Whatsoever you ask in My Name with believing hearts, My Father in Heaven will grant unto you according to His Will."

Father, may Your Will be done. Help us accept Your Will, for You truly know far better than we what is best for us.

We believe, Lord. Help us! Please help us overcome our disbelief.

AMEN.

About the Author

Pastor Russell B. Greene is the son of a Lutheran minister and a native of Berne, New York. His "home church" was St. Paul's Lutheran Church.

He attended Paul Smiths College in Paul Smiths, New York. He also attended Wagner College in Staten Island, New York, where he received his Bachelor of Arts degree in 1955. He received his Bachelor of Divinity and Master of Divinity degrees from Mount Airy Lutheran Theological Seminary in Philadelphia, Pennsylvania. He received his Master of Science degree in Education from Wagner College in 1962.

In 1956, Pastor Greene served as Chaplain to over 3,000 Boy Scouts at Camp Delmont in Pennsylvania.

From 1957 to 1962, he served as Assistant Pastor at Trinity Lutheran Church in Staten Island, New York. During this time he was involved in the development and establishment of the Trinity Lutheran Parochial School. He also served on various committees in connection with the educational and youth ministry of the local church and the Church at large.

He presented a series of sermons on NBC television and radio, and he played an active role in the Protestant Council's "Dial-A-Prayer" program.

Pastor Greene commenced his pastorate at Good Shepherd Lutheran Church in Norwalk, Connecticut, on September 1, 1962.

Under his leadership, a new church and fellowship hall were constructed. The new house of worship was dedicated to the glory of God in 1967.

In addition to his ministry at Good Shepherd, he served as a chaplain in the Norwalk Hospital, chaplain of several nursing homes, and was chairman of WNLK Radio - Family Devotions.

He was also an active member of the Norwalk Kiwanis Club, of which he was chaplain, and chairman of the Support the Churches Committee.

He has served as chaplain at New England Synod conventions as well as chaplain for innumerable group gatherings. He served as secretary of the Southern Connecticut District of the New England Synod of the ELCA

(Evangelical Lutheran Church of America) for seven years, as well as serving on the New England Synod Nominating Committee and the New England Synod Committee of Resolution and Counsel. He has been engaged in numerous ecumenical events. He served on the board of directors of the Connecticut Counseling Center, Inc. — a vital resource for various Connecticut communities it serves — providing evaluation, medical counseling, and referral serves to those battling mental illness and substance abuse.

He is a Son of the American Revolution. He served as chaplain of the Roger Sherman Branch #5, CTSSAR.

In his retirement, he resides with his wife Marion in Norwalk, Connecticut, and remains active with his friends and family. He spends his time writing, reading and counseling.